Ready, Set, JUMBLE®

Let the Games Begin!

Henri Arnold,
Bob Lee,
and
Mike Argirion

TRIUMPH
BOOKS

This book is available in quantity at special discounts
for your group or organization.

For further information, contact:

Triumph Books
542 South Dearborn Street
Suite 750
Chicago, Illinois 60605
(312) 939-3330
Fax (312) 663-3557

Printed in U.S.A.

ISBN: 978-1-60078-133-0

Design by Sue Knopf

CONTENTS

Ready, Set,

JUMBLE®

Classic Puzzles

JUMBLE®

Unscramble these four Jumbles, one letter to each square, to form four ordinary words.

MOPET

PHEES

YOTHER

BELTOT

WHAT ALL THOSE SUGGESTIONS ABOUT IMPROVING THE DOUGHNUT BUSINESS SEEMED TO HAVE.

Now arrange the circled letters to form the surprise answer, as suggested by the above cartoon.

Print answer here ⬡⬡⬡⬡⬡ IN ⬡⬡⬡⬡

JUMBLE®

Unscramble these four Jumbles, one letter to each square, to form four ordinary words.

COUFS

LAKBY

DORRIT

YALWEE

Sorry, I've changed my mind

PRIVATE

DICTIONARY

WHAT A HYPHEN PERMITS YOU TO DO.

Now arrange the circled letters to form the surprise answer, as suggested by the above cartoon.

Print answer here ⬡⬡⬡⬡⬡ YOUR ⬡⬡⬡⬡

JUMBLE®

Unscramble these four Jumbles, one letter to each square, to form four ordinary words.

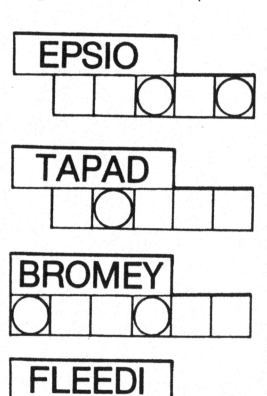

EPSIO

TAPAD

BROMEY

FLEEDI

HOW A STAG IS OFTEN FORCED TO RUN.

Now arrange the circled letters to form the surprise answer, as suggested by the above cartoon.

Print answer here FOR " ⬡⬡⬡⬡ " ⬡⬡⬡⬡

JUMBLE®

Unscramble these four Jumbles, one letter to each square, to form four ordinary words.

RAUZE

BETER

SURWAL

INGROI

There goes his promotion

SOME PEOPLE MIGHT RISE HIGHER IF THEY'D LEARN TO DO THIS.

Now arrange the circled letters to form the surprise answer, as suggested by the above cartoon.

Print answer here

JUMBLE®

Unscramble these four Jumbles, one letter to each square, to form four ordinary words.

INBAC

THILE

PLOGES

REPHEL

Er-ah-er, d-do y-you I-love me?

ONE ISN'T SURE TO SAY IT.

Now arrange the circled letters to form the surprise answer, as suggested by the above cartoon.

Print answer here

6

JUMBLE.

Unscramble these four Jumbles, one letter to each square, to form four ordinary words.

AMFER

POAYS

YAQUES

RECHOM

DID YOU HEAR MY LAST JOKE?

Now arrange the circled letters to form the surprise answer, as suggested by the above cartoon.

Print answer here " I  "

JUMBLE®

Unscramble these four Jumbles, one letter to each square, to form four ordinary words.

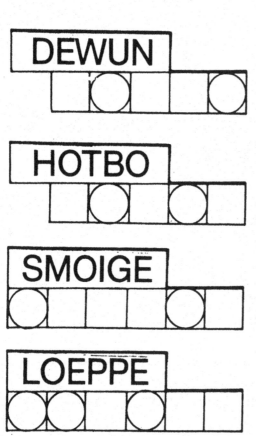

DEWUN

HOTBO

SMOIGE

LOEPPE

Don't ever darken my door again!

WHAT A GUY WHO ACTS LIKE A HEEL SHOULD BE.

Now arrange the circled letters to form the surprise answer, as suggested by the above cartoon.

Print answer here

8

JUMBLE®

Unscramble these four Jumbles, one letter to each square, to form four ordinary words.

TAIMY

HAWRT

NETOED

DECSON

Now arrange the circled letters to form the surprise answer, as suggested by the above cartoon.

Print answer here ◯◯◯◯ " ◯◯◯◯◯ "

JUMBLE.

Unscramble these four Jumbles, one letter to each square, to form four ordinary words.

NIGTY

SHACO

ENBATE

BLOWEB

HOW PEOPLE SAW THINGS AFTER THE DISCOVERY OF ELECTRICITY.

Now arrange the circled letters to form the surprise answer, as suggested by the above cartoon.

Print answer here IN A ☐☐☐ ☐☐☐☐☐

JUMBLE®

Unscramble these four Jumbles, one letter to
each square, to form four ordinary words.

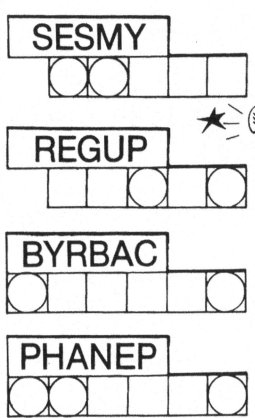

SESMY

REGUP

BYRBAC

PHANEP

WHAT FLATFEET
CAN BE.

Now arrange the circled letters to form the
surprise answer, as suggested by the above
cartoon.

Print answer here THE " ⬡⬡⬡⬡⬡ ⬡⬡⬡⬡⬡⬡ "

JUMBLE®

Unscramble these four Jumbles, one letter to each square, to form four ordinary words.

RUTYL

SONOW

UPDELD

CALARI

Who can tell me what life is like here— and here?

WHAT THE EARTH'S TWO POLAR REGIONS ARE.

Now arrange the circled letters to form the surprise answer, as suggested by the above cartoon.

Print answer here A

JUMBLE®

Unscramble these four Jumbles, one letter to
each square, to form four ordinary words.

ZAWLT

CLOON

SOOMER

DOUSIT

WHO SAW THE
DINOSAUR ENTERING
THE RESTAURANT?

Now arrange the circled letters to form the
surprise answer, as suggested by the above
cartoon.

Print answer here   THE

JUMBLE®

Unscramble these four Jumbles, one letter to each square, to form four ordinary words.

BITHA

RIVOS

ENSICC

YARDOP

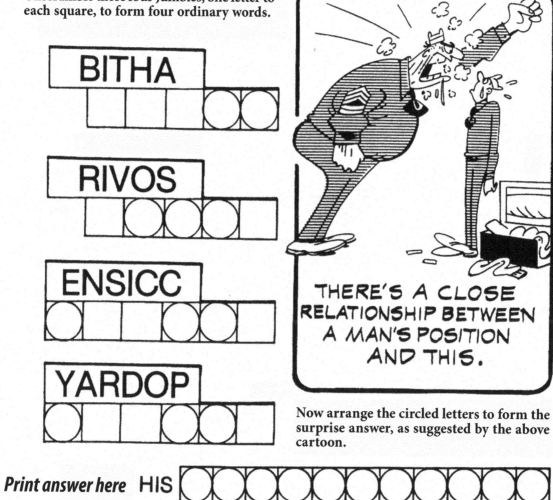

THERE'S A CLOSE
RELATIONSHIP BETWEEN
A MAN'S POSITION
AND THIS.

Now arrange the circled letters to form the surprise answer, as suggested by the above cartoon.

Print answer here HIS ⬡⬡⬡⬡⬡⬡⬡⬡⬡⬡⬡⬡

JUMBLE®

Unscramble these four Jumbles, one letter to each square, to form four ordinary words.

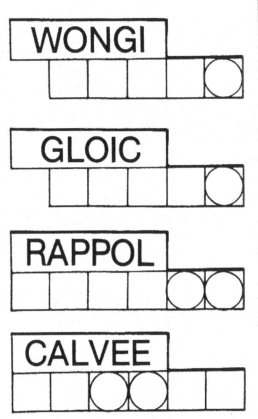

WONGI

GLOIC

RAPPOL

CALVEE

MEANT THE DISAPPEARANCE OF THE CARRIAGE.

Now arrange the circled letters to form the surprise answer, as suggested by the above cartoon.

Print answer here THE " ☐☐☐ ☐☐☐ "

15

JUMBLE®

Unscramble these four Jumbles, one letter to each square, to form four ordinary words.

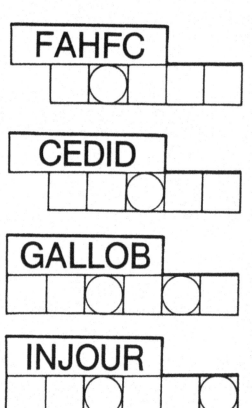

FAHFC

CEDID

GALLOB

INJOUR

Let's join the activities!

A STICK-IN-THE-MUD FOUND IN A SHIP.

Now arrange the circled letters to form the surprise answer, as suggested by the above cartoon.

Print answer here THE

16

JUMBLE®

Unscramble these four Jumbles, one letter to each square, to form four ordinary words.

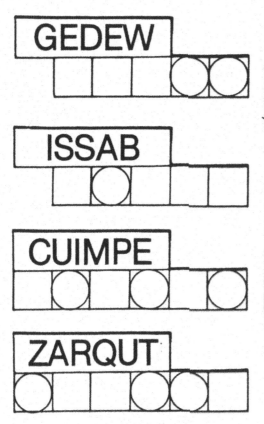

GEDEW

ISSAB

CUIMPE

ZARQUT

WHAT TANTRUMS ARE FOR SOME KIDS THESE DAYS.

Now arrange the circled letters to form the surprise answer, as suggested by the above cartoon.

Print answer here ☐☐☐☐☐ THE ☐☐☐☐

17

JUMBLE®

Unscramble these four Jumbles, one letter to
each square, to form four ordinary words.

CORUC

TOSOP

DUMPIO

HIRDBY

WHEN IT COMES
TO LOVE, AN
ENGAGEMENT
RING IS THIS.

Now arrange the circled letters to form the
surprise answer, as suggested by the above
cartoon.

Print answer here A "◯◯◯" ◯◯◯◯◯◯◯

JUMBLE®

Unscramble these four Jumbles, one letter to each square, to form four ordinary words.

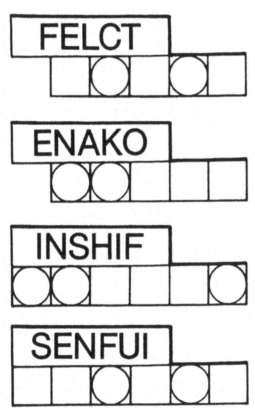

FELCT

ENAKO

INSHIF

SENFUI

IT WAS OFF-SEASON FOR FISHING, WHICH IS WHY THE SHERIFF MADE IT THIS.

Now arrange the circled letters to form the surprise answer, as suggested by the above cartoon.

Print answer here "☐○○ - ○○○○ - ○○"

JUMBLE

Unscramble these four Jumbles, one letter to each square, to form four ordinary words.

BEDRY

CLAWR

REBAVE

MANALY

WHAT THE BANK ROBBER GOT WHEN THE SECURITY SYSTEM SOUNDED.

Now arrange the circled letters to form the surprise answer, as suggested by the above cartoon.

Print answer here "  "

20

JUMBLE®

Unscramble these four Jumbles, one letter to
each square, to form four ordinary words.

LEAGE

YARIF

CLARNE

RALOPP

WHAT TO DO WHEN
THE BAROMETER
FALLS.

Now arrange the circled letters to form the
surprise answer, as suggested by the above
cartoon.

*Print
answer
here*   ◯◯◯◯◯◯◯ THE ◯◯◯◯

JUMBLE®

Unscramble these four Jumbles, one letter to each square, to form four ordinary words.

KEREC

MALUB

YERRSH

DAIMWY

WHAT THE BEE-KEEPER SAID ON AN UNUSUALLY HOT DAY.

Now arrange the circled letters to form the surprise answer, as suggested by the above cartoon.

Print answer here   IT'S "◯◯◯◯◯" ◯◯◯◯

PUZZLE
22

JUMBLE®

Unscramble these four Jumbles, one letter to each square, to form four ordinary words.

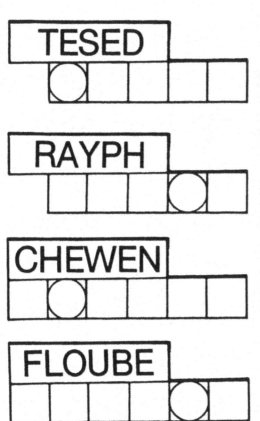

TESED

RAYPH

CHEWEN

FLOUBE

Go ahead -- you deserve a raise

He won't bite you

WHAT THE SIGN ON THE DOOR OF OPPORTUNITY READS.

Now arrange the circled letters to form the surprise answer, as suggested by the above cartoon.

Print answer here " ◯◯◯◯ "

23

JUMBLE®

Unscramble these four Jumbles, one letter to each square, to form four ordinary words.

YAGIL

WHISS

VERGAN

HIPLAC

THEY RESIDED ON THE ROOF BECAUSE THEY LOVED THIS.

Now arrange the circled letters to form the surprise answer, as suggested by the above cartoon.

Print answer here "  "

JUMBLE®

Unscramble these four Jumbles, one letter to each square, to form four ordinary words.

PAWMS

⬜⬜⬜⬜⬜

NEEMY

⬜⬜⬜⬜⬜

THALEC

⬜⬜⬜⬜⬜⬜

PHOONC

⬜⬜⬜⬜⬜⬜

THERE'S A STRANGE DRIP IN THE BASEMENT. SHALL I CALL THE PLUMBER?

Now arrange the circled letters to form the surprise answer, as suggested by the above cartoon.

Print answer here "⬜⬜, ⬜⬜⬜ ⬜⬜⬜⬜⬜!"

JUMBLE®

Unscramble these four Jumbles, one letter to each square, to form four ordinary words.

ZIERP

ORNED

RACCES

MADAKS

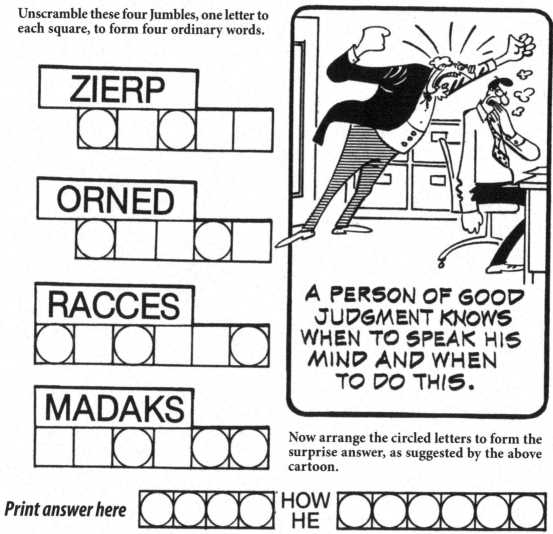

A PERSON OF GOOD JUDGMENT KNOWS WHEN TO SPEAK HIS MIND AND WHEN TO DO THIS.

Now arrange the circled letters to form the surprise answer, as suggested by the above cartoon.

Print answer here

HOW HE

JUMBLE®

Unscramble these four Jumbles, one letter to each square, to form four ordinary words.

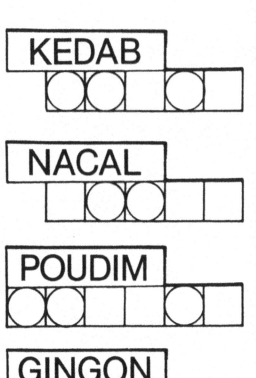

KEDAB

NACAL

POUDIM

GINGON

WHAT THE JOB OF DELIVERING PARCELS SOME—TIMES IS.

Now arrange the circled letters to form the surprise answer, as suggested by the above cartoon.

Print answer here

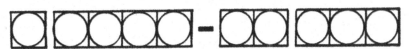

JUMBLE®

Unscramble these four Jumbles, one letter to each square, to form four ordinary words.

SHWIK

GUCOH

TRENGY

HOKOUN

This is where you get off

REDUCING SALON

I should have gone directly to the office

IN ORDER TO PLEASE HIS WIFE, HE RELUCTANTLY AGREED TO GO THERE.

Now arrange the circled letters to form the surprise answer, as suggested by the above cartoon.

Print answer here ☐☐☐ OF "☐☐☐☐☐"
HIS

JUMBLE®

Unscramble these four Jumbles, one letter to each square, to form four ordinary words.

KEHRI

LAMDY

RAKNEC

DABBIE

I mustn't gossip so much

THE ACROBAT WAS THE ONLY GUY WHO KNEW HOW TO TALK ABOUT HIMSELF---

Now arrange the circled letters to form the surprise answer, as suggested by the above cartoon.

Print answer here

HIS OWN

JUMBLE®

Unscramble these four Jumbles, one letter to
each square, to form four ordinary words.

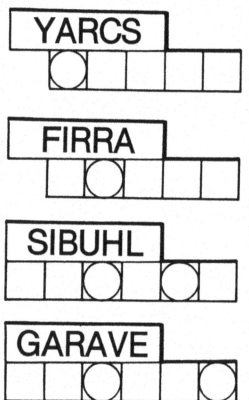

YARCS

FIRRA

SIBUHL

GARAVE

TONIGHT
LONGFELLOW
- - - -
SHAKESPEARE
10 ROUNDS

WHAT CAME BETWEEN
THOSE TWO POETS
TURNED PROFES -
SIONAL BOXERS?

Now arrange the circled letters to form the
surprise answer, as suggested by the above
cartoon.

Print answer here

JUMBLE®

Unscramble these four Jumbles, one letter to each square, to form four ordinary words.

EUQIR

NOAGY

YADDLE

GENNIE

WHAT KIND OF AN EXPERIENCE IS IT TO TRAVEL BY FLYING CARPET?

Now arrange the circled letters to form the surprise answer, as suggested by the above cartoon.

Print answer here   A ⟨◯◯◯◯◯◯⟩ ONE

JUMBLE

Unscramble these four Jumbles, one letter to each square, to form four ordinary words.

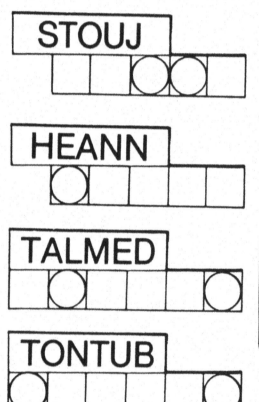

STOUJ

HEANN

TALMED

TONTUB

THAT BLONDE SURE HAS SOME-THING THAT'LL KNOCK YOUR EYE OUT---

Now arrange the circled letters to form the surprise answer, as suggested by the above cartoon.

Print answer here A

Unscramble these four Jumbles, one letter to each square, to form four ordinary words.

CEHEN

YUNTI

ENJUKT

HESKAN

Sure is long-winded when it comes to writing

IN THE PEN DOING A LONG SENTENCE.

Now arrange the circled letters to form the surprise answer, as suggested by the above cartoon.

Print answer here

33

JUMBLE®

Unscramble these four Jumbles, one letter to each square, to form four ordinary words.

BUNGE

COVAL

REPIME

YEMMAH

Ah, that's for me!

COULD THIS BEER BE LARGE?

Now arrange the circled letters to form the surprise answer, as suggested by the above cartoon.

Print answer here " ◯◯◯◯◯ "

JUMBLE®

Unscramble these four Jumbles, one letter to each square, to form four ordinary words.

SHLYP

UPCOE

DUSARI

ELGANT

WHAT THOSE OLD—TIME VETERINARIANS USED TO MAKE.

Now arrange the circled letters to form the surprise answer, as suggested by the above cartoon.

Print answer here "◯◯◯◯◯" ◯◯◯◯◯◯

JUMBLE®

Unscramble these four Jumbles, one letter to each square, to form four ordinary words.

TIMAD

DACKE

YAFULT

CADILP

Better slow down

A CAREFUL DRIVER IS THE GUY WHO HAS JUST SEEN THE CAR IN FRONT OF HIM GET THIS.

Now arrange the circled letters to form the surprise answer, as suggested by the above cartoon.

Print answer here

JUMBLE®

Unscramble these four Jumbles, one letter to each square, to form four ordinary words.

LODDY

KNOTE

EXVONC

DIALIN

Maybe he can help us out

WHY THE JURY ASKED TO SEE THE ACCUSED SAFE-CRACKER AGAIN.

Now arrange the circled letters to form the surprise answer, as suggested by the above cartoon.

Print answer here

THEY WERE ☐☐☐☐ " ☐☐☐☐☐☐ "

JUMBLE®

Unscramble these four Jumbles, one letter to each square, to form four ordinary words.

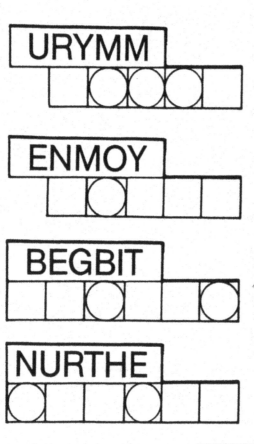

URYMM

ENMOY

BEGBIT

NURTHE

WHAT MIGHT TOM DO WHEN HIS CAR BREAKS DOWN?

Now arrange the circled letters to form the surprise answer, as suggested by the above cartoon.

Print answer here  " "

JUMBLE

Unscramble these four Jumbles, one letter to each square, to form four ordinary words.

OTTOH

ZYZID

NOBBIB

EXCOIB

YAK YAK
YAK YAK

AN "ADDICTION" TO THIS CAN CAUSE SOME PEOPLE TO BECOME SLEEPY.

Now arrange the circled letters to form the surprise answer, as suggested by the above cartoon.

Print answer here " ◯◯◯◯◯◯◯ "

JUMBLE®

Unscramble these four Jumbles, one letter to each square, to form four ordinary words.

YEMSS

SURVI

DOHOKE

CRESIB

WHAT THAT AMOROUS PITCHER KNEW HOW TO THROW BEST.

Now arrange the circled letters to form the surprise answer, as suggested by the above cartoon.

Print answer here

JUMBLE®

Unscramble these four Jumbles, one letter to
each square, to form four ordinary words.

ENFEC

MEPIR

TOEGEA

ODONEL

WHAT MIGHT GO ON
INSIDE A COMPASS?

Now arrange the circled letters to form the
surprise answer, as suggested by the above
cartoon.

Print
answer
here

"_____ _____"

JUMBLE®

Unscramble these four Jumbles, one letter to each square, to form four ordinary words.

NOWVE

PIMBL

FORFET

LYROOP

This is going to help my career

WHAT YOU ARE WHEN YOU HAVE SOMETHING ON THE BOSS.

Now arrange the circled letters to form the surprise answer, as suggested by the above cartoon.

Print answer here " ◯◯◯◯◯   ◯◯◯◯◯◯ "

JUMBLE.

Unscramble these four Jumbles, one letter to
each square, to form four ordinary words.

LUDEE

EKQUA

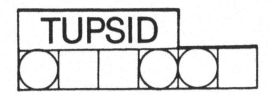

TUPSID

IPSOME

WHAT THE
GARBAGEMAN
SAID HE WAS.

Now arrange the circled letters to form the
surprise answer, as suggested by the above
cartoon.

Print answer here   AT
HER   " ◯◯◯◯◯◯◯◯ "

43

JUMBLE®

Unscramble these four Jumbles, one letter to each square, to form four ordinary words.

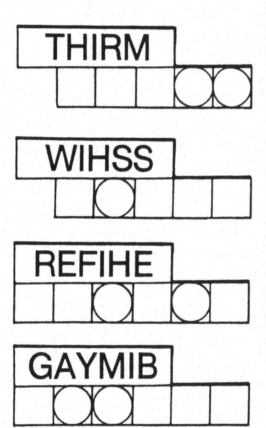

THIRM

WIHSS

REFIHE

GAYMIB

JEWELRY

HOW TO FIND OUT IF YOUR WATCH IS GAINING.

Now arrange the circled letters to form the surprise answer, as suggested by the above cartoon.

Print answer here

44

44

JUMBLE®

Unscramble these four Jumbles, one letter to each square, to form four ordinary words.

TILEE

LOFEN

RYNTIG

CALHUN

WHEN HE FINALLY GOT THE FIRE-PLACE WORKING, SHE WAS THIS.

Now arrange the circled letters to form the surprise answer, as suggested by the above cartoon.

Print answer here " ◯◯◯◯◯ – ◯◯◯◯ "

45

JUMBLE

Unscramble these four Jumbles, one letter to
each square, to form four ordinary words.

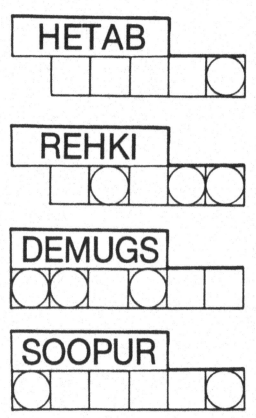

HETAB

REHKI

DEMUGS

SOOPUR

They seem to know
what they're doing

WHEN THE COWBOYS
FINISHED BRANDING
THEM, THE COWS
WERE REALLY THIS.

Now arrange the circled letters to form the
surprise answer, as suggested by the above
cartoon.

Print answer here " ◯◯◯◯◯◯◯◯◯ "

Ready, Set, JUMBLE®

Daily Puzzles

JUMBLE®

Unscramble these four Jumbles, one letter to each square, to form four ordinary words.

DALGE

JEGUD

LEWBIA

CATTIN

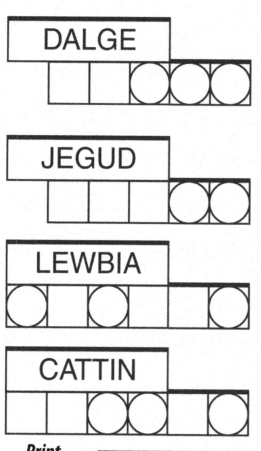

This is war!

Hear hear

ON STRIKE

WHAT THE WORKERS DID TO GET A PAY RAISE.

Now arrange the circled letters to form the surprise answer, as suggested by the above cartoon.

Print answer here

" " A

JUMBLE®

Unscramble these four Jumbles, one letter to each square, to form four ordinary words.

GALIE

VAHEY

BINTAD

BIFCAR

Hi, how you doin'?

O.K. How 'bout you?

A LONG WORD THAT DOESN'T MEAN A LOT.

Now arrange the circled letters to form the surprise answer, as suggested by the above cartoon.

Print answer here

JUMBLE®

Unscramble these four Jumbles, one letter to each square, to form four ordinary words.

YUTIN

TEYIP

RATTAR

LYROOP

Print answer here

Better get to work – that's one-way glass

THE SALES MANAGER FAVORED A WINDOW OF ---

Now arrange the circled letters to form the surprise answer, as suggested by the above cartoon.

49

JUMBLE®

Unscramble these four Jumbles, one letter to
each square, to form four ordinary words.

ADURF

AFESH

PRINGY

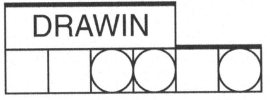

DRAWIN

We've got
to hide
our find

In the cave

HOW THEY KEPT
THE MUMMY AT
THE SECRET DIG.

Now arrange the circled letters to form the
surprise answer, as suggested by the above
cartoon.

*Print
answer
here*

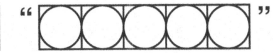

JUMBLE®

Unscramble these four Jumbles, one letter to each square, to form four ordinary words.

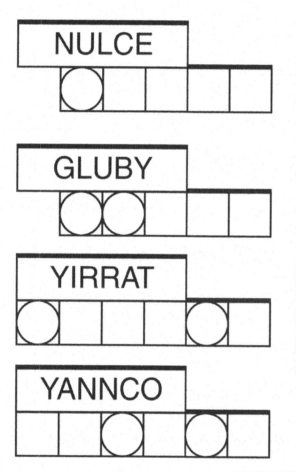

NULCE

GLUBY

YIRRAT

YANNCO

I can't keep up

WHAT THE OVER-WORKED COOK EXPERIENCED.

Now arrange the circled letters to form the surprise answer, as suggested by the above cartoon.

Print answer here " ◯◯◯◯ " ◯◯◯

JUMBLE®

Unscramble these four Jumbles, one letter to each square, to form four ordinary words.

NELLK

STRYT

HUTORF

DAIMWY

ACME BANK

TOUGH FOR A NIGHT WATCHMAN TO AVOID STEALING.

Now arrange the circled letters to form the surprise answer, as suggested by the above cartoon.

Print answer here

53

JUMBLE®

Unscramble these four Jumbles, one letter to each square, to form four ordinary words.

YOWND

NEALK

CANTIG

GUTONI

I hope it doesn't rain

MOMS WERE DOING THIS YEARS BEFORE COMPU-TERIZED LIVING.

Now arrange the circled letters to form the surprise answer, as suggested by the above cartoon.

Print answer here

JUMBLE®

Unscramble these four Jumbles, one letter to
each square, to form four ordinary words.

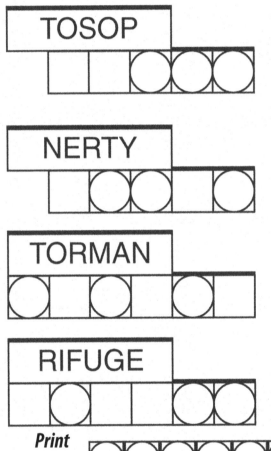

TOSOP

NERTY

TORMAN

RIFUGE

How do I
love thee,
let me count …

RECITING A VERSE
CAN TURN A
MORNING RUN
INTO THIS.

Now arrange the circled letters to form the
surprise answer, as suggested by the above
cartoon.

*Print
answer
here*

IN

JUMBLE®

Unscramble these four Jumbles, one letter to each square, to form four ordinary words.

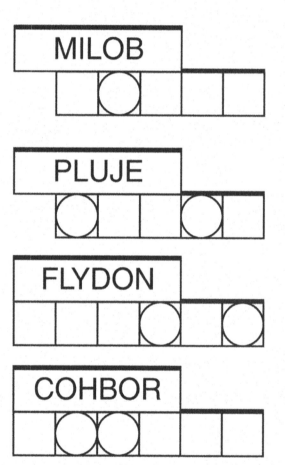

MILOB

PLUJE

FLYDON

COHBOR

I won! I'm so excited!

THE WINNING DRIVER TURNED HIS VICTORY LAP INTO THIS.

Now arrange the circled letters to form the surprise answer, as suggested by the above cartoon.

Print answer here   A " ◯◯◯ " ◯◯◯◯

JUMBLE®

Unscramble these four Jumbles, one letter to each square, to form four ordinary words.

HACTY

DRECY

SLYJUT

ZIEFER

I make my own. It's a fast meal

WHY THE MEDICAL STUDENT LIKED HAM.

Now arrange the circled letters to form the surprise answer, as suggested by the above cartoon.

Print answer here

IT'S ☐☐☐☐☐ "☐☐☐☐☐"

JUMBLE®

Unscramble these four Jumbles, one letter to each square, to form four ordinary words.

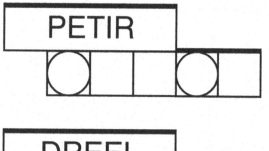

PETIR

DREEL

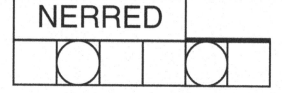

NERRED

YERRAF

She marches to her own drummer

THE SAUCY ACTRESS' FANS THOUGHT SHE WAS ---

Now arrange the circled letters to form the surprise answer, as suggested by the above cartoon.

Print answer here

"   -   "

JUMBLE®

Unscramble these four Jumbles, one letter to
each square, to form four ordinary words.

NOIBS

MABLY

JEERTS

SHONCE

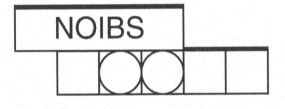

Might as well practice

HONK
HONK

THE BRASS BAND
TURNED THE
TRAFFIC TIE-UP
INTO THIS.

Now arrange the circled letters to form the
surprise answer, as suggested by the above
cartoon.

*Print
answer
here* A "◯◯◯" ◯◯◯◯◯◯◯

59

JUMBLE®

Unscramble these four Jumbles, one letter to
each square, to form four ordinary words.

EGGOR

TIELE

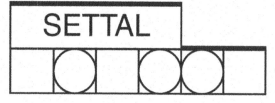

SETTAL

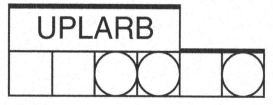

UPLARB

Stay awake, it's
getting better

WHAT HE HOPED
THE MOVIE WOULD
TURN INTO.

Now arrange the circled letters to form the
surprise answer, as suggested by the above
cartoon.

Print
answer   A
here

JUMBLE®

Unscramble these four Jumbles, one letter to each square, to form four ordinary words.

TUDOO

VEFER

CRIMTE

YARPIT

PIPE DOWN!

Now where did I put that chalk?

EASY TO LOSE WITH A ROWDY CLASS.

Now arrange the circled letters to form the surprise answer, as suggested by the above cartoon.

Print answer here

JUMBLE®

Unscramble these four Jumbles, one letter to each square, to form four ordinary words.

RACCK

NAIGG

JINNOE

REVONG

Chapter 11, here we come

CLOSING

ALL PRICES SLASHED

WHAT HE CON-SIDERED HIS NEARLY BANK-RUPT BUSINESS.

Now arrange the circled letters to form the surprise answer, as suggested by the above cartoon.

Print answer A here " ⬡⬡⬡⬡⬡ " ⬡⬡⬡⬡⬡⬡⬡

Unscramble these four Jumbles, one letter to
each square, to form four ordinary words.

HACOP

DEBIA

STEGAK

TANUBE

That's four in a
row. You're going
downhill

WHERE THE BOXER
ENDED UP WHEN
HE STARTED
LOSING.

Now arrange the circled letters to form the
surprise answer, as suggested by the above
cartoon.

*Print
answer
here* ON
THE " "

63

JUMBLE®

Unscramble these four Jumbles, one letter to each square, to form four ordinary words.

UGLLY

INYAR

DAILNG

BANACA

He has to get up earlier than us

WHAT IT TAKES TO BE AN ARMY BUGLER.

Now arrange the circled letters to form the surprise answer, as suggested by the above cartoon.

Print answer here A " ⬡⬡⬡⬡⬡⬡⬡ "

64

JUMBLE®

Unscramble these four Jumbles, one letter to each square, to form four ordinary words.

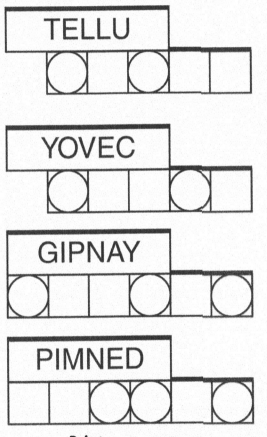

TELLU

YOVEC

GIPNAY

PIMNED

Why don't you go in?   Look at all the money I save

Ye Barber Shoppe

HE AVOIDED THE FANCY BARBER-SHOP BECAUSE HE DIDN'T WANT TO - - - -

Now arrange the circled letters to form the surprise answer, as suggested by the above cartoon.

Print answer here

JUMBLE®

Unscramble these four Jumbles, one letter to each square, to form four ordinary words.

FETAC

GUNED

DOITUS

MESHEC

I'm still hungry

Where did all the food go?

WHAT IT TOOK
FOR THE BOARDER
TO FINISH
DINNER.

Now arrange the circled letters to form the surprise answer, as suggested by the above cartoon.

Print answer here " "

JUMBLE®

Unscramble these four Jumbles, one letter to each square, to form four ordinary words.

TANCE

TEPIN

YUCLOD

TUDOUG

You've ruined these steaks. Get out!

WHY THE BUTCHER WAS FIRED.

Now arrange the circled letters to form the surprise answer, as suggested by the above cartoon.

Print answer here   HE ⬡⬡⬡⬡⬡⬡ ' ⬡ " ⬡⬡⬡ " IT

JUMBLE®

Unscramble these four Jumbles, one letter to
each square, to form four ordinary words.

RICHA

SAGYS

KONVIE

GABLEN

WHY DID THE
PATRONS
FREQUENT
THE HAPPY HOUR?

Now arrange the circled letters to form the
surprise answer, as suggested by the above
cartoon.

Print
answer FOR "⬭⬭⬭ - ⬭⬭⬭⬭⬭"
here

JUMBLE®

Unscramble these four Jumbles, one letter to each square, to form four ordinary words.

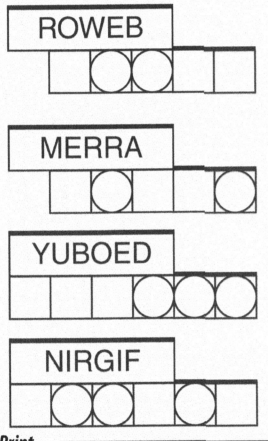

ROWEB

MERRA

YUBOED

NIRGIF

This job will pay some bills

WHAT THE YOUNG ELECTRICIAN DID WHEN HE WAS BROKE.

Now arrange the circled letters to form the surprise answer, as suggested by the above cartoon.

Print answer here "◯◯◯◯◯" FOR ◯◯◯◯◯

JUMBLE®

Unscramble these four Jumbles, one letter to each square, to form four ordinary words.

URYMM

LURTY

CHUPIC

BYSTUL

Just adding some finishing touches

AN ART STUDENT WILL DO THIS BEFORE AN EXAM.

Now arrange the circled letters to form the surprise answer, as suggested by the above cartoon.

Print answer here

JUMBLE®

Unscramble these four Jumbles, one letter to each square, to form four ordinary words.

LOXET

NYWEL

MAANSE

CLITIE

I'm a little short

Pay me next week

WHAT THE STORE OWNER GAVE THE LADDER BUYER.

Now arrange the circled letters to form the surprise answer, as suggested by the above cartoon.

Print answer here   AN

JUMBLE®

Unscramble these four Jumbles, one letter to
each square, to form four ordinary words.

BODUT

HEWEL

SNOOPI

RYVETS

Oops!

Clean up and get out!

WHERE THE
WAITER LANDED
WHEN HE DROPPED
THE TUREEN.

Now arrange the circled letters to form the
surprise answer, as suggested by the above
cartoon.

Print answer here

JUMBLE®

Unscramble these four Jumbles, one letter to each square, to form four ordinary words.

NOOHR

YARCS

THAILG

FLEMUF

What kind of champagne do you have?

I'd like some caviar

WHAT THE CHARTER PILOT CONSID-ERED THE PLANE-LOAD OF SOCIETY MATRONS.

Now arrange the circled letters to form the surprise answer, as suggested by the above cartoon.

Print answer here

A ⬡⬡⬡⬡⬡⬡ OF "⬡⬡⬡⬡⬡"

73

JUMBLE®

Unscramble these four Jumbles, one letter to each square, to form four ordinary words.

TIBEF

KORBO

RORTER

RETTUL

Raise you a hundred

Too rich for me

HE WON THE POKER HAND BE-CAUSE HE WAS ----

Now arrange the circled letters to form the surprise answer, as suggested by the above cartoon.

Print answer here

A

PUZZLE
73

JUMBLE®

Unscramble these four Jumbles, one letter to each square, to form four ordinary words.

RABDN

GUSET

RIGDIF

FLOAFY

I'm not impressed -- slow down!

WHAT SHE CON-SIDERED HIS HIGH-SPEED EXIT FROM THE FREEWAY.

Now arrange the circled letters to form the surprise answer, as suggested by the above cartoon.

Print answer here A " ⬡⬡⬡⬡ ⬡⬡⬡ "

75

JUMBLE®

Unscramble these four Jumbles, one letter to each square, to form four ordinary words.

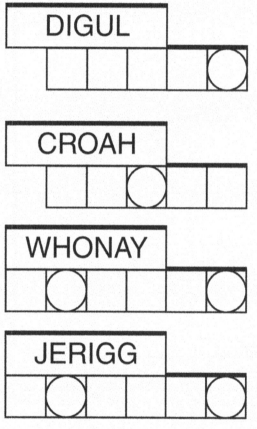

DIGUL

CROAH

WHONAY

JERIGG

Hmm--I've decided these two are the best

HOW THE ART CONTEST ENDED UP.

Now arrange the circled letters to form the surprise answer, as suggested by the above cartoon.

Print answer here ☐☐ A " ☐☐☐☐ "

76

JUMBLE®

Unscramble these four Jumbles, one letter to each square, to form four ordinary words.

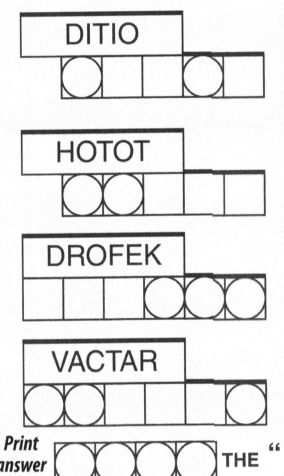

DITIO

HOTOT

DROFEK

VACTAR

You did it, J.B.

He saved the company

WHAT THE CEO DID WHEN THE LOAN WAS APPROVED.

Now arrange the circled letters to form the surprise answer, as suggested by the above cartoon.

Print answer here

THE " "

JUMBLE®

Unscramble these four Jumbles, one letter to each square, to form four ordinary words.

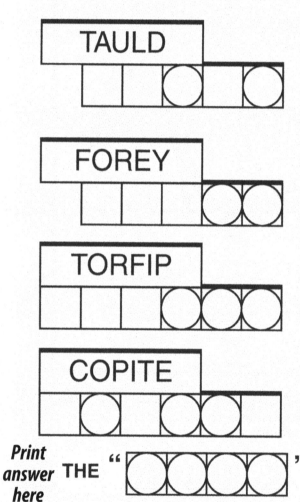

TAULD

FOREY

TORFIP

COPITE

She looks gorgeous

She has something borrowed

IMPORTANT TO WEAR TO HER WEDDING.

Now arrange the circled letters to form the surprise answer, as suggested by the above cartoon.

Print answer here   THE "⬡⬡⬡⬡"   ⬡⬡⬡⬡⬡⬡⬡

JUMBLE®

Unscramble these four Jumbles, one letter to
each square, to form four ordinary words.

MEHRY

ETTIL

IBBADE

GRENED

You're a big boy, Butch,
you have to be brave

WHAT THE NURSE
DID WHEN SHE
GAVE THE BODY
BUILDER A SHOT.

Now arrange the circled letters to form the
surprise answer, as suggested by the above
cartoon.

Print
answer SHE "◯◯◯◯◯◯◯" ◯◯◯
here

JUMBLE®

Unscramble these four Jumbles, one letter to
each square, to form four ordinary words.

LOYKE

NOCOL

NIGDIH

SINUGE

Nothing like a cozy fire

WHAT SHE DID
BEFORE GOING
ONLINE ON A
COLD NIGHT.

Now arrange the circled letters to form the
surprise answer, as suggested by the above
cartoon.

Print answer here " ⃝⃝⃝⃝⃝⃝ " ⃝⃝

JUMBLE®

Unscramble these four Jumbles, one letter to each square, to form four ordinary words.

DIPTE

NALBA

KENART

TUCLED

That's $6.05. Careful, it's fragile

EASY TO DO THESE DAYS WITH A TEN DOLLAR BILL.

Now arrange the circled letters to form the surprise answer, as suggested by the above cartoon.

Print answer here

81

JUMBLE®

Unscramble these four Jumbles, one letter to
each square, to form four ordinary words.

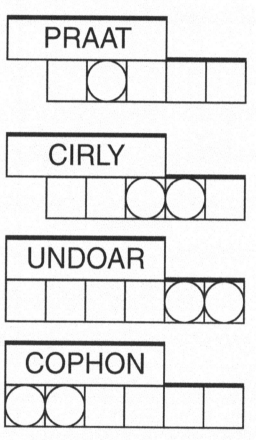

PRAAT

CIRLY

UNDOAR

COPHON

STRIKE!

DESPITE THE
NOISE, EASY TO
HEAR IN A
BOWLING ALLEY.

Now arrange the circled letters to form the
surprise answer, as suggested by the above
cartoon.

Print answer here   A

JUMBLE®

Unscramble these four Jumbles, one letter to
each square, to form four ordinary words.

GYNIL

OCTIX

LAIHNE

LURSEY

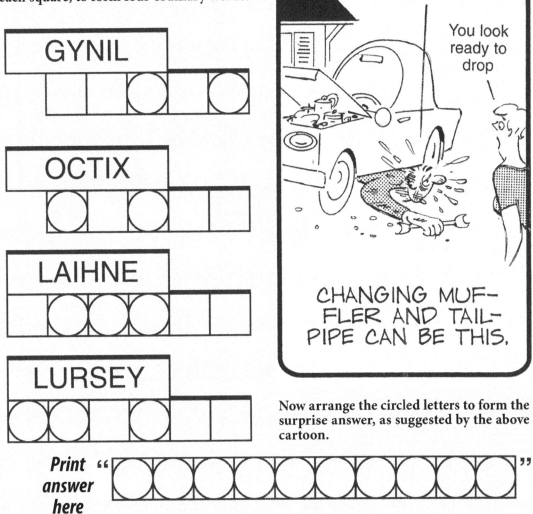

Whew, tough job

You look
ready to
drop

CHANGING MUF-
FLER AND TAIL-
PIPE CAN BE THIS.

Now arrange the circled letters to form the
surprise answer, as suggested by the above
cartoon.

Print
answer
here

" "

JUMBLE®

Unscramble these four Jumbles, one letter to each square, to form four ordinary words.

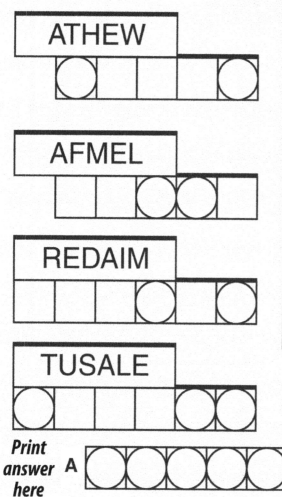

ATHEW

AFMEL

REDAIM

TUSALE

It's 5 o'clock

Mine's always fast or slow

BUYING A CHEAP WATCH CAN TURN OUT TO BE ----

Now arrange the circled letters to form the surprise answer, as suggested by the above cartoon.

Print answer here

A  OF "  "

JUMBLE®

Unscramble these four Jumbles, one letter to each square, to form four ordinary words.

TOOBA

POEMT

KHONUO

LADJIE

I'll take the whole shipment

Excellent

Another big order for Sam

SELLING PRUNES TURNED OUT TO BE THIS.

Now arrange the circled letters to form the surprise answer, as suggested by the above cartoon.

Print answer here A " ⬡⬡⬡⬡ " ⬡⬡⬡

JUMBLE®

Unscramble these four Jumbles, one letter to
each square, to form four ordinary words.

REIND

CEENF

UMRAIB

KEENAW

She's sole support
of her family

WHAT SHE TURNED
INTO WHEN HER
LOAF OF RYE
WON THE BLUE
RIBBON.

Now arrange the circled letters to form the
surprise answer, as suggested by the above
cartoon.

*Print
answer
here* THE ☐☐☐☐☐ ☐☐☐☐☐☐

JUMBLE®

Unscramble these four Jumbles, one letter to each square, to form four ordinary words.

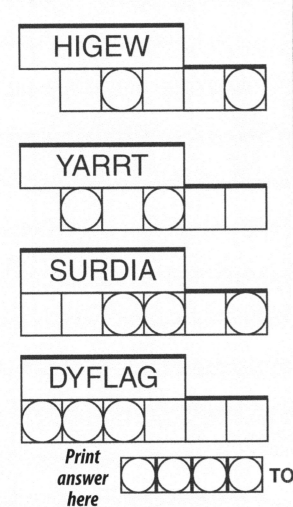

HIGEW

YARRT

SURDIA

DYFLAG

I can't remember all of this

STUDYING FOR A DIFFICULT NUTRITION EXAM CAN BE----

Now arrange the circled letters to form the surprise answer, as suggested by the above cartoon.

Print answer here

TO "   "

JUMBLE®

Unscramble these four Jumbles, one letter to each square, to form four ordinary words.

COUFS

SHURC

CHABLE

SARATY

You all did a great job

YOU MIGHT CALL THAT FINE STU-DENT DRAMA THIS.

Now arrange the circled letters to form the surprise answer, as suggested by the above cartoon.

Print answer here A "◯◯◯◯◯" ◯◯◯

JUMBLE®

Unscramble these four Jumbles, one letter to each square, to form four ordinary words.

GREME

BUIME

WINDOS

YAHMME

Here's your pay. Nice job

WHAT THE BUSBOY RECEIVED FOR HIS MAXIMUM EFFORT.

Now arrange the circled letters to form the surprise answer, as suggested by the above cartoon.

Print answer here

A

JUMBLE®

Unscramble these four Jumbles, one letter to
each square, to form four ordinary words.

GORCA

FLABE

GHOTUB

CODJUN

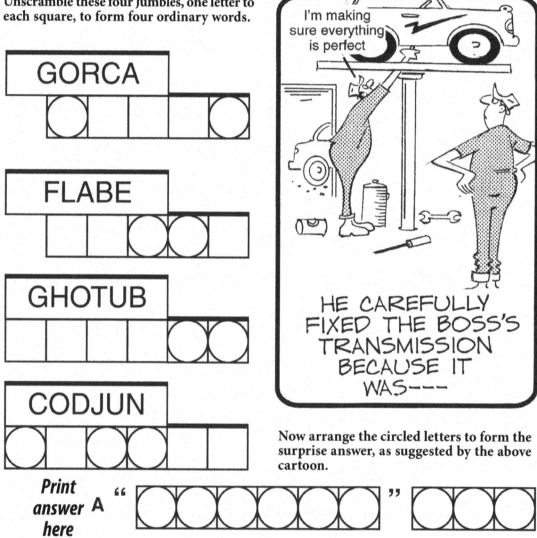

I'm making
sure everything
is perfect

HE CAREFULLY
FIXED THE BOSS'S
TRANSMISSION
BECAUSE IT
WAS---

Now arrange the circled letters to form the
surprise answer, as suggested by the above
cartoon.

Print
answer A   "   "
here

JUMBLE®

Unscramble these four Jumbles, one letter to each square, to form four ordinary words.

KWONN

NUBOD

SYPEDE

MOUFAS

THE ELEVATOR OPERATOR WASN'T BOTHERED BY THIS AT THE STOCK EXCHANGE.

Now arrange the circled letters to form the surprise answer, as suggested by the above cartoon.

Print answer here

91

JUMBLE®

Unscramble these four Jumbles, one letter to each square, to form four ordinary words.

SEROU

JETEC

FEENID

SAFTIE

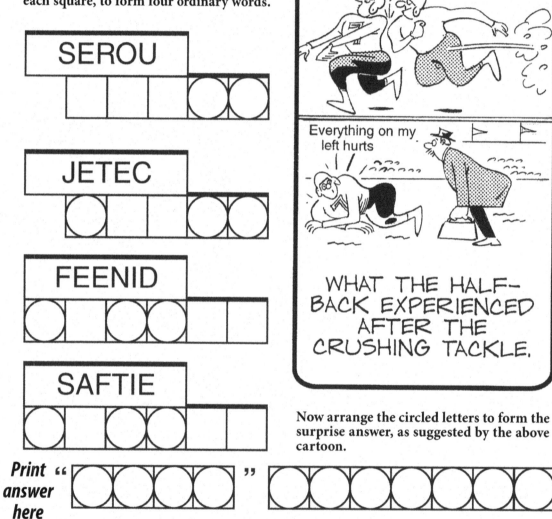

Everything on my left hurts

WHAT THE HALF-BACK EXPERIENCED AFTER THE CRUSHING TACKLE.

Now arrange the circled letters to form the surprise answer, as suggested by the above cartoon.

Print answer here " ⬡⬡⬡⬡ " ⬡⬡⬡⬡⬡⬡⬡⬡

Unscramble these four Jumbles, one letter to each square, to form four ordinary words.

ODARR

YIRNB

YALWEE

UMLUTT

That's a lot of cash

Business has been good

BANK

WHY DID THE CROOKED CLEANER TAKE THE MONEY TO THE BANK?

Now arrange the circled letters to form the surprise answer, as suggested by the above cartoon.

Print answer here

TO " ⬡⬡⬡⬡⬡⬡⬡ " ⬡⬡

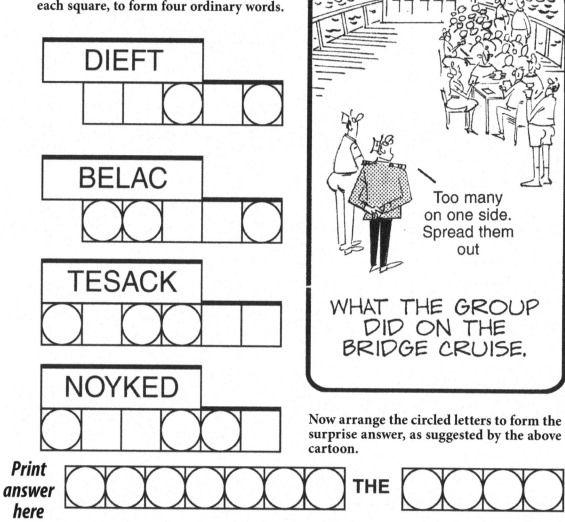

JUMBLE®

Unscramble these four Jumbles, one letter to each square, to form four ordinary words.

DIEFT

BELAC

TESACK

NOYKED

Too many on one side. Spread them out

WHAT THE GROUP DID ON THE BRIDGE CRUISE.

Now arrange the circled letters to form the surprise answer, as suggested by the above cartoon.

Print answer here

⬡⬡⬡⬡⬡⬡⬡ **THE** ⬡⬡⬡⬡

94

JUMBLE®

Unscramble these four Jumbles, one letter to
each square, to form four ordinary words.

PONCA

THOIS

TARDIO

DIPTIE

Did not!   Did so!

I missed
the turnoff

Quiet
down!

WHERE THE
SQUABBLING KIDS
DROVE DAD.

Now arrange the circled letters to form the
surprise answer, as suggested by the above
cartoon.

Print
answer **TO**
here

JUMBLE®

Unscramble these four Jumbles, one letter to each square, to form four ordinary words.

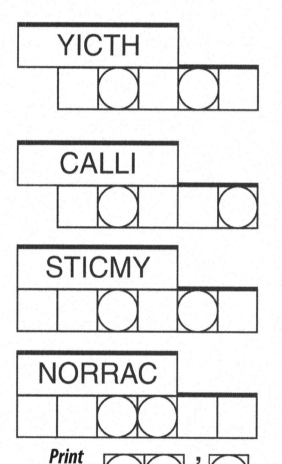

YICTH

CALLI

STICMY

NORRAC

Easier than I thought

Nice job

WHAT HE SAID WHEN HE MADE A BELT IN CRAFTS CLASS.

Now arrange the circled letters to form the surprise answer, as suggested by the above cartoon.

Print answer here ⬡⬡ ' ⬡ A " ⬡⬡⬡⬡⬡ "

JUMBLE®

Unscramble these four Jumbles, one letter to each square, to form four ordinary words.

RUSUY

OTAFO

TURBET

VOONCY

How about kids?

Hey, weren't you the champ?

WHEN THE PRIZE-FIGHTER BECAME A CENSUS TAKER HE WAS ---

Now arrange the circled letters to form the surprise answer, as suggested by the above cartoon.

Print answer here ⬡⬡⬡ **FOR THE** ⬡⬡⬡⬡⬡⬡

JUMBLE®

Unscramble these four Jumbles, one letter to
each square, to form four ordinary words.

GOTEB

INCCY

TEROTT

MAIROH

I got a good price

WHAT HE
BROUGHT HOME
WHEN HE TOOK
THE PIGS
TO MARKET.

Now arrange the circled letters to form the
surprise answer, as suggested by the above
cartoon.

Print answer here

JUMBLE®

Unscramble these four Jumbles, one letter to each square, to form four ordinary words.

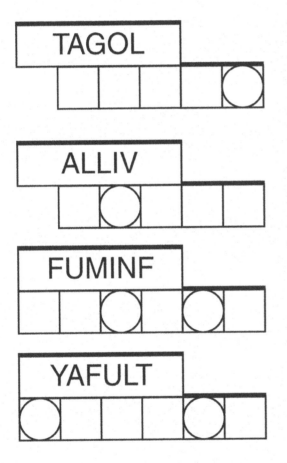

TAGOL

ALLIV

FUMINF

YAFULT

Nothing works ... I quit!

A TOUGH JIGSAW PUZZLE CAN LEAD TO THIS.

Now arrange the circled letters to form the surprise answer, as suggested by the above cartoon.

Print answer here A

PUZZLE
98

JUMBLE®

Unscramble these four Jumbles, one letter to
each square, to form four ordinary words.

LIVIG

CRAID

OLDBOY

UCCSAU

How do they
keep warm?

WHAT THE HIPPIES
CONSIDERED THE
IGLOO.

Now arrange the circled letters to form the
surprise answer, as suggested by the above
cartoon.

Print answer here " ◯◯◯◯ " ◯◯◯◯

100

JUMBLE®

Unscramble these four Jumbles, one letter to each square, to form four ordinary words.

CYREM

ALCKO

SWORDY

SNUFIL

You've got a call

Not now, I'm busy

A GOOD PHOTOG-
RAPHER WILL
DO THIS.

Now arrange the circled letters to form the surprise answer, as suggested by the above cartoon.

Print answer here " ◯◯◯◯◯ " ON HIS ◯◯◯◯

JUMBLE®

Unscramble these four Jumbles, one letter to each square, to form four ordinary words.

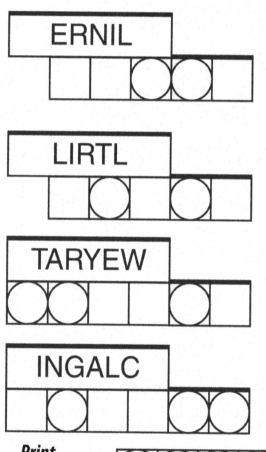

ERNIL

LIRTL

TARYEW

INGALC

KEEP OFF

Hey, get off the grass

WHAT THE MONITOR TURNED INTO WHEN THE STUDENTS BROKE THE RULES.

Now arrange the circled letters to form the surprise answer, as suggested by the above cartoon.

Print answer here   THE ⬡⬡⬡⬡ ⬡⬡⬡⬡⬡⬡⬡

102

JUMBLE®

Unscramble these four Jumbles, one letter to
each square, to form four ordinary words.

NAVER

EUDLE

NATILE

TORRCE

I want my
money back

Sorry, all sales
are final

WHAT THE GRO-
CER GAVE HER
WHEN THE FRUIT
SPOILED.

Now arrange the circled letters to form the
surprise answer, as suggested by the above
cartoon.

Print
answer
here

A

JUMBLE®

Unscramble these four Jumbles, one letter to each square, to form four ordinary words.

YIKTT

CILIY

EXFLAN

YASQUE

Better hurry, looks like it's going to pour

WHAT WAS NEEDED WHEN THE OLD BUGGY FINALLY BROKE DOWN.

Now arrange the circled letters to form the surprise answer, as suggested by the above cartoon.

Print answer here A

JUMBLE®

Unscramble these four Jumbles, one letter to each square, to form four ordinary words.

TOOPH

EXIDO

YETHIG

GOCHUR

WHAT THE MOUNTAIN CLIMBERS PAID TO REACH THE SUMMIT.

Now arrange the circled letters to form the surprise answer, as suggested by the above cartoon.

Print answer here A " ⬡⬡⬡⬡ " ⬡⬡⬡⬡⬡

JUMBLE®

Unscramble these four Jumbles, one letter to each square, to form four ordinary words.

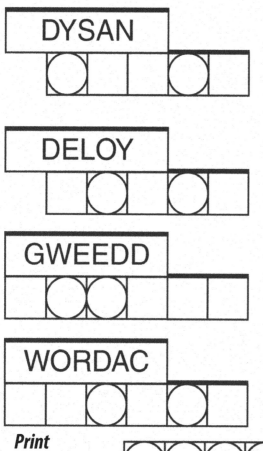

DYSAN

DELOY

GWEEDD

WORDAC

4 to 1 favorite

You're nuts.
5 to 2
underdog

WHY THE
BOOKIES FOUGHT.

Now arrange the circled letters to form the surprise answer, as suggested by the above cartoon.

Print answer here   THEY ⬡⬡⬡⬡ AT " ⬡⬡⬡⬡ "

JUMBLE®

Unscramble these four Jumbles, one letter to each square, to form four ordinary words.

WUNDE

THILG

YALMIN

LARVEM

How 'bout dinner and a movie?

Positive-ly not

WHAT THE PHO-
TOGRAPHER
ENDED UP WITH
WHEN HE MADE
A PASS.

Now arrange the circled letters to form the surprise answer, as suggested by the above cartoon.

Print answer here A

107

JUMBLE®

Unscramble these four Jumbles, one letter to each square, to form four ordinary words.

EGGOU

RACZE

SHUBAM

DRIMBO

He's got more signals than a coach

TO THE BALL PLAYERS, THE CONDUCTOR'S MUSIC STAND WAS THIS.

Now arrange the circled letters to form the surprise answer, as suggested by the above cartoon.

Print answer here A " ◯◯◯◯◯◯ " ◯◯◯◯◯

108

JUMBLE®

Unscramble these four Jumbles, one letter to
each square, to form four ordinary words.

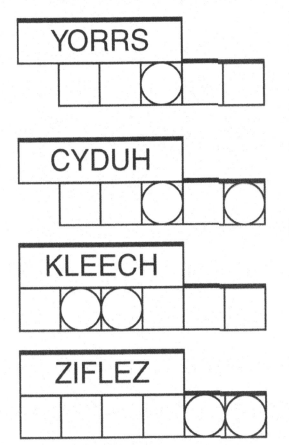

YORRS

CYDUH

KLEECH

ZIFLEZ

I can make
this as
good as new

EASY TO DO AT
A JUNKYARD.

Now arrange the circled letters to form the
surprise answer, as suggested by the above
cartoon.

Print answer here " ⬡⬡ - ⬡⬡⬡⬡⬡ "

109

JUMBLE®

Unscramble these four Jumbles, one letter to each square, to form four ordinary words.

YODIL

ALVIA

YARNLE

ULDDEC

Whew! I'm going home and hit the sack

WHAT HE DID AFTER WORKING AROUND THE CLOCK.

Now arrange the circled letters to form the surprise answer, as suggested by the above cartoon.

Print
answer
here

IT
A   "   "

JUMBLE.

Unscramble these four Jumbles, one letter to
each square, to form four ordinary words.

NAYDD

PEWID

EDDOMO

LOUBES

It's very
depressing

WHERE THEY
ENDED UP WHEN
THE NEARBY
PROPERTY BECAME
A LANDFILL.

Now arrange the circled letters to form the
surprise answer, as suggested by the above
cartoon.

*Print
answer
here*

IN
THE

" "

JUMBLE®

Unscramble these four Jumbles, one letter to each square, to form four ordinary words.

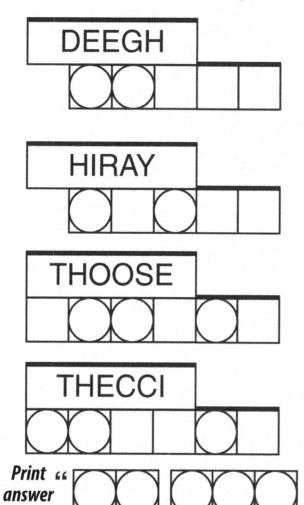

DEEGH

HIRAY

THOOSE

THECCI

HE LISTENED TO HIS FAVORITE SONG WHEN DOING HIS GAR-DENING.

Now arrange the circled letters to form the surprise answer, as suggested by the above cartoon.

Print answer here " ⬭⬭ ⬭⬭⬭ , ⬭⬭ ⬭⬭⬭ "

JUMBLE.

Unscramble these four Jumbles, one letter to each square, to form four ordinary words.

HITEL

DAFEM

BADCUT

CHORCS

WHAT MOM MADE JUNIOR DO WHEN HE TRIED TO DUCK PIANO PRACTICE.

Now arrange the circled letters to form the surprise answer, as suggested by the above cartoon.

Print answer here ⬡⬡⬡⬡ THE ⬡⬡⬡⬡⬡

113

JUMBLE®

Unscramble these four Jumbles, one letter to each square, to form four ordinary words.

WREEF
◯ ◯ ◯

LUKKS
◯ ◯ ◯

SHAWCE
◯ ◯ ◯

FOISSY
◯ ◯

Never got a ticket

A GOOD WAY TO RECEIVE A SAFE DRIVING AWARD.

Now arrange the circled letters to form the surprise answer, as suggested by the above cartoon.

Print answer here BE ◯◯◯◯◯ - ◯◯◯◯

JUMBLE®

Unscramble these four Jumbles, one letter to each square, to form four ordinary words.

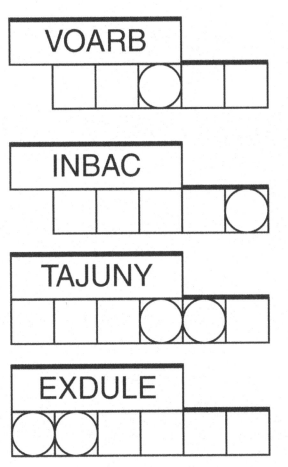

VOARB

INBAC

TAJUNY

EXDULE

You deserve a spanking for disappearing

WHAT HE GOT WHEN HE DIS-OBEYED MOM AT THE BEACH.

Now arrange the circled letters to form the surprise answer, as suggested by the above cartoon.

Print answer here " 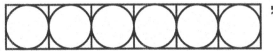 "

JUMBLE®

Unscramble these four Jumbles, one letter to each square, to form four ordinary words.

YERME

USEAT

PERUSH

DEGLUC

Isn't it what you wanted done?

CUTTING DOWN THOSE BEAUTIFUL TREES LEFT THEM LIKE THIS.

Now arrange the circled letters to form the surprise answer, as suggested by the above cartoon.

Print answer here " ◯◯◯◯◯◯◯ "

JUMBLE®

Unscramble these four Jumbles, one letter to each square, to form four ordinary words.

KETOS

SARBS

SMUTTO

SESCUN

We're under so much pressure

I haven't slept in days

THE MEDICAL STUDENTS SAID THEIR FINAL EXAMS WERE ----

Now arrange the circled letters to form the surprise answer, as suggested by the above cartoon.

Print answer here " ☐☐☐☐☐☐ " ☐☐☐☐☐

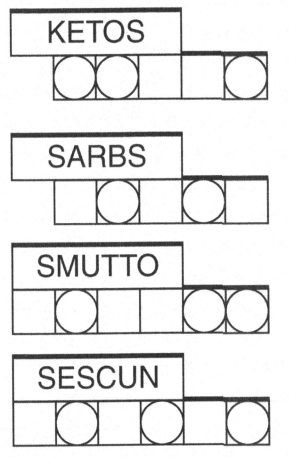

JUMBLE®

Unscramble these four Jumbles, one letter to
each square, to form four ordinary words.

RINPT

UNDET

DIONIE

FLOUBE

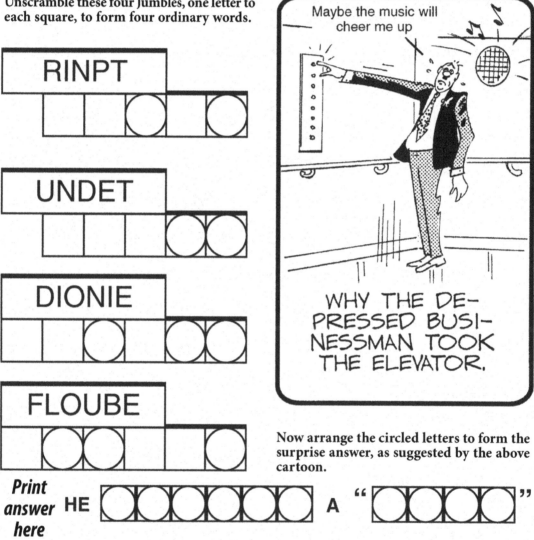

Maybe the music will cheer me up

WHY THE DE-
PRESSED BUSI-
NESSMAN TOOK
THE ELEVATOR.

Now arrange the circled letters to form the
surprise answer, as suggested by the above
cartoon.

Print
answer   HE ⬚⬚⬚⬚⬚⬚ A " ⬚⬚⬚⬚ "
here

118

JUMBLE®

Unscramble these four Jumbles, one letter to each square, to form four ordinary words.

VANIE

BORNI

ENGOUT

LOOGGI

I find it fulfilling

I'll take this one

MAKING VASES WAS HIS WAY OF DOING THIS.

Now arrange the circled letters to form the surprise answer, as suggested by the above cartoon.

Print answer here " ☐☐☐☐☐☐ " A ☐☐☐☐☐☐

JUMBLE ®

Unscramble these four Jumbles, one letter to each square, to form four ordinary words.

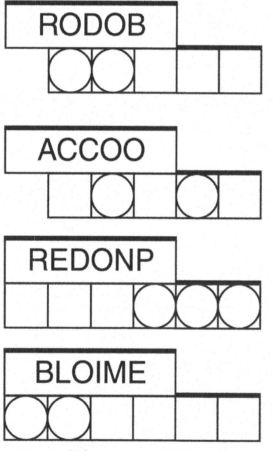

RODOB

ACCOO

REDONP

BLOIME

It's lonely. How're the kids?

WHAT A SALESMAN GETS WHEN HE'S ON THE ROAD.

Now arrange the circled letters to form the surprise answer, as suggested by the above cartoon.

Print answer here

 AND

JUMBLE®

Unscramble these four Jumbles, one letter to each square, to form four ordinary words.

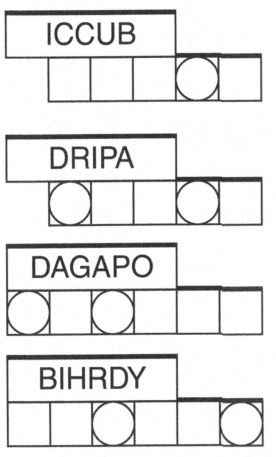

ICCUB

DRIPA

DAGAPO

BIHRDY

Whee -- some fun, huh?

WHEN HE SPLASHED HER AT THE POOL PARTY SHE THOUGHT HE WAS ---

Now arrange the circled letters to form the surprise answer, as suggested by the above cartoon.

Print answer here A

JUMBLE®

Unscramble these four Jumbles, one letter to each square, to form four ordinary words.

WEPOR

TOUHY

VORREF

REFLOG

Don't bother us now

How many stops to Midville, Pop?

WHAT THE CON-
DUCTOR TOLD
THE OBNOXIOUS
PASSENGERS.

Now arrange the circled letters to form the surprise answer, as suggested by the above cartoon.

Print answer here

TO

JUMBLE®

Unscramble these four Jumbles, one letter to each square, to form four ordinary words.

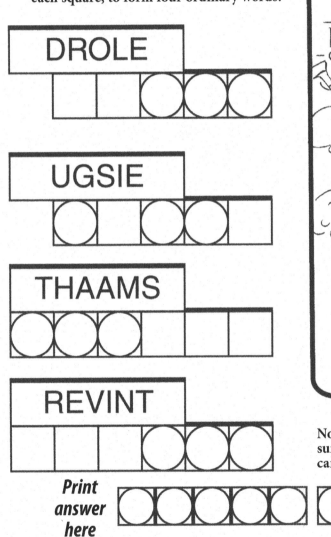

DROLE

UGSIE

THAAMS

REVINT

You're coming along very well

WHAT HE MADE WHEN HE BEGAN RUNNING TO GET FIT.

Now arrange the circled letters to form the surprise answer, as suggested by the above cartoon.

Print answer here

JUMBLE®

Unscramble these four Jumbles, one letter to each square, to form four ordinary words.

DRAYT

NILTE

GRAFUL

LYSEEP

I don't like its looks

THE PUB OWNER THREW OUT THE STATUE BECAUSE IT WAS ---

Now arrange the circled letters to form the surprise answer, as suggested by the above cartoon.

Print answer here " ◯◯◯◯◯◯◯◯◯◯ "

JUMBLE®

Unscramble these four Jumbles, one letter to each square, to form four ordinary words.

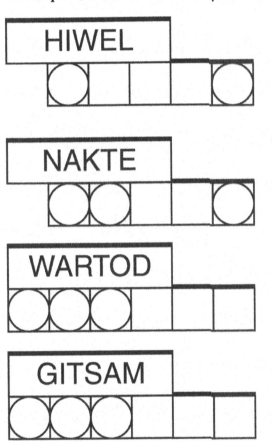

HIWEL

NAKTE

WARTOD

GITSAM

I have to work on the abs

WHAT HAPPENED TO THE BODY-BUILDER'S SHAPE WHEN HE GAINED WEIGHT.

Now arrange the circled letters to form the surprise answer, as suggested by the above cartoon.

Print answer here IT

125

JUMBLE®

Unscramble these four Jumbles, one letter to
each square, to form four ordinary words.

GUCOH

TIFAH

CUSTOC

MUSCLY

We've got mustard,
onions, relish,
tomatoes, ketchup ...

Gimme,
I'm starved!

WHAT HE WANTED
ON HIS HOT DOG.

Now arrange the circled letters to form the
surprise answer, as suggested by the above
cartoon.

Print answer here

JUMBLE®

Unscramble these four Jumbles, one letter to
each square, to form four ordinary words.

WENIT

NYSAP

LINGES

RUBECH

It's
too
cold

I need
fresh air

TOUGH FOR SOME
TO SLEEP
WITHOUT THIS.

Now arrange the circled letters to form the
surprise answer, as suggested by the above
cartoon.

Print answer here A

JUMBLE®

Unscramble these four Jumbles, one letter to each square, to form four ordinary words.

CHOAV

HUSBY

LARULP

FACEEF

I can do it for $10,000

Oh, yeah? Scram!

WHAT THE HOUSE PAINTER GOT WHEN HIS BID WAS TOO HIGH.

Now arrange the circled letters to form the surprise answer, as suggested by the above cartoon.

Print answer here

THE "  "

128

JUMBLE®

Unscramble these four Jumbles, one letter to each square, to form four ordinary words.

VORLE

FRYOT

DITORR

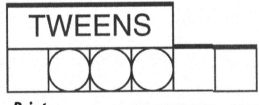
TWEENS

Perfect. Modest, but fashionable

WHERE THE DESIGNER PRE-FERRED THE HEMLINE.

Now arrange the circled letters to form the surprise answer, as suggested by the above cartoon.

Print answer here

JUMBLE®

Unscramble these four Jumbles, one letter to each square, to form four ordinary words.

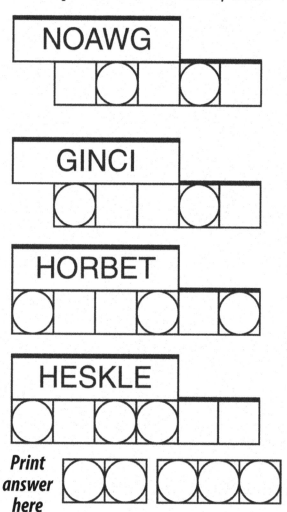

NOAWG

GINCI

HORBET

HESKLE

Ooops! Back soon

WHERE DID THE
CLUMSY DISH-
WASHER GO?

Now arrange the circled letters to form the surprise answer, as suggested by the above cartoon.

Print answer here

" "

JUMBLE®

Unscramble these four Jumbles, one letter to each square, to form four ordinary words.

CLATH
◯◯◯□□

LIGUT
◯□□◯◯

LAISEY
◯◯◯□□□

LANNID
□◯□□◯◯

WINNING THE
CHAMPIONSHIP
LEFT THE
BASKETBALL
TEAM DOING THIS.

Now arrange the circled letters to form the surprise answer, as suggested by the above cartoon.

Print answer here

◯◯◯◯◯◯◯◯ ◯◯◯◯

JUMBLE®

Unscramble these four Jumbles, one letter to each square, to form four ordinary words.

LEVED

OONNI

YIVERF

BLOWEB

I can't believe it

Wow! Way to go!

HOW HE FELT WHEN HE ROLLED A PERFECT GAME.

Now arrange the circled letters to form the surprise answer, as suggested by the above cartoon.

Print answer here

JUMBLE

Unscramble these four Jumbles, one letter to
each square, to form four ordinary words.

DRIOF

YASES

FITANN

FALLOR

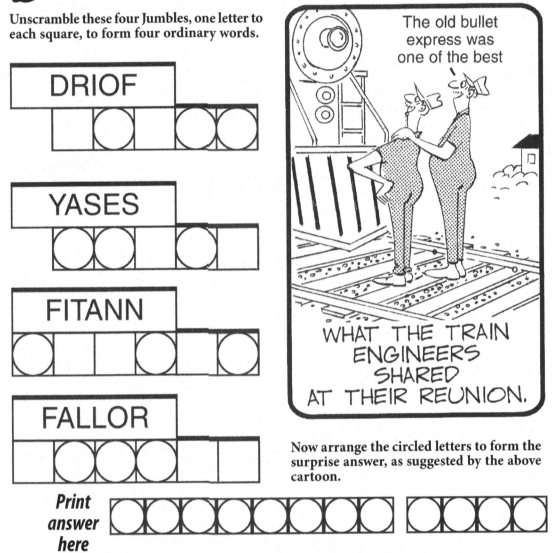

The old bullet
express was
one of the best

WHAT THE TRAIN
ENGINEERS
SHARED
AT THEIR REUNION.

Now arrange the circled letters to form the
surprise answer, as suggested by the above
cartoon.

*Print
answer
here*

133

JUMBLE®

Unscramble these four Jumbles, one letter to each square, to form four ordinary words.

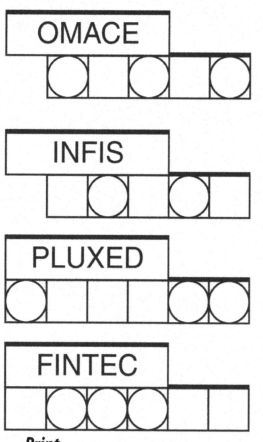

OMACE

INFIS

PLUXED

FINTEC

Everything's getting more expensive

We'll have to cut down on the groceries

BILL

BILL

THIS CAN PUT YOUR BUDGET IN DISREPAIR.

Now arrange the circled letters to form the surprise answer, as suggested by the above cartoon.

Print answer here   A " ⬡⬡⬡⬡⬡ " ⬡⬡⬡⬡⬡⬡

JUMBLE®

Unscramble these four Jumbles, one letter to each square, to form four ordinary words.

DAPIL

YAILG

EVITLY

CHEWEN

That dopey bird doesn't know where he is

WHAT THE HOMING PIGEON DID WHEN IT LOST ITS WAY.

Now arrange the circled letters to form the surprise answer, as suggested by the above cartoon.

Print answer here   " ◯◯◯◯◯◯◯ "   ◯◯

135

JUMBLE®

Unscramble these four Jumbles, one letter to each square, to form four ordinary words.

DESTE

LAVEE

VAHDLE

PHATAY

Pssst, want to buy a watch cheap?

WHAT THE CROOKED PEDDLER OFFERED ON THE SUNNY BEACH.

Now arrange the circled letters to form the surprise answer, as suggested by the above cartoon.

Print answer here

A " ◯◯◯◯◯ " ◯◯◯◯

136

JUMBLE®

Unscramble these four Jumbles, one letter to
each square, to form four ordinary words.

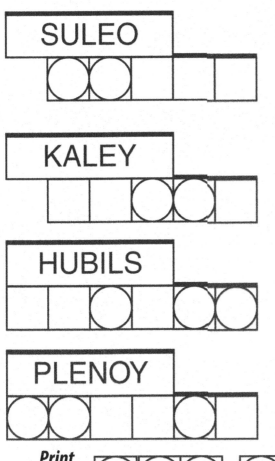

SULEO

KALEY

HUBILS

PLENOY

I've been on the
job for 8 hours

HOW THE BAR-
TENDER FELT
AT THE END
OF HIS SHIFT.

Now arrange the circled letters to form the
surprise answer, as suggested by the above
cartoon.

Print
answer
here

JUMBLE®

Unscramble these four Jumbles, one letter to each square, to form four ordinary words.

NUGOY

UNORM

ENVEAL

NURTAT

It's going to be a huge hit

CASTING CALL

WHAT THE ACTOR HOPED THE PLAY ABOUT A MARATHON WOULD HAVE.

Now arrange the circled letters to form the surprise answer, as suggested by the above cartoon.

Print answer here A

JUMBLE®

Unscramble these four Jumbles, one letter to each square, to form four ordinary words.

NURSP

SATHY

MAZECE

INOUSC

Can I get it?

Only if you can pay for it

$20

WHAT HE NEEDED TO DO WHEN HE WANTED THE HALLOWEEN MASK.

Now arrange the circled letters to form the surprise answer, as suggested by the above cartoon.

Print answer here

⬡⬡⬡⬡⬡ UP ⬡⬡⬡⬡

JUMBLE®

Unscramble these four Jumbles, one letter to each square, to form four ordinary words.

CLEEX

LYKIM

GERDED

LASSIA

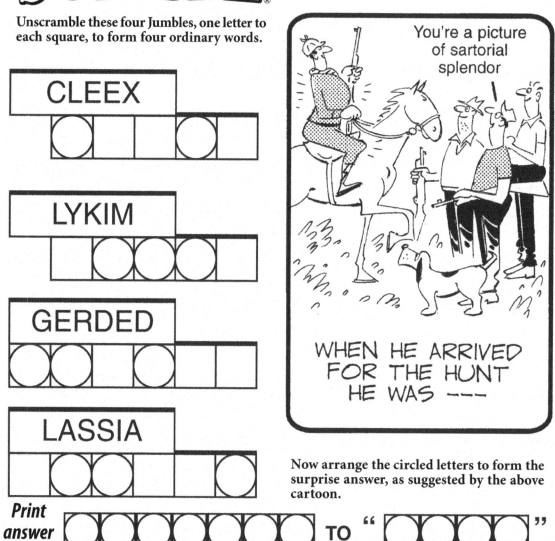

You're a picture of sartorial splendor

WHEN HE ARRIVED FOR THE HUNT HE WAS ---

Now arrange the circled letters to form the surprise answer, as suggested by the above cartoon.

Print answer here

[ ][ ][ ][ ][ ][ ][ ] TO " [ ][ ][ ][ ] "

JUMBLE®

Unscramble these four Jumbles, one letter to each square, to form four ordinary words.

HIWSS

PRIGE

SLAVIE

NIFTIE

I eat every other day

WHAT A CRASH DIET CAN LEAD TO.

Now arrange the circled letters to form the surprise answer, as suggested by the above cartoon.

Print answer here " ◯◯◯◯ " ◯◯◯◯◯◯

JUMBLE®

Unscramble these four Jumbles, one letter to each square, to form four ordinary words.

BOLEN

GORRI

UNTHAG

VISPLE

Who did this?

He did it

He did it

WHAT MOM CAME UP WITH WHEN THE CARPET WAS MYSTERIOUSLY STAINED.

Now arrange the circled letters to form the surprise answer, as suggested by the above cartoon.

Print answer here A " ◯◯◯◯◯◯◯◯ "

142

JUMBLE

Unscramble these four Jumbles, one letter to
each square, to form four ordinary words.

GALEE

GAMLE

ALOONG

SHARTH

Here's your
order, pilgrim

He thinks he's
John Wayne

SERVED BY THE
ASPIRING ACTOR
AT THE BREAK-
FAST COUNTER.

Now arrange the circled letters to form the
surprise answer, as suggested by the above
cartoon.

Print answer here " ○○○ " AND ○○○○

JUMBLE®

Unscramble these four Jumbles, one letter to each square, to form four ordinary words.

RITHM

SYTUM

SMUQIR

KLUNIE

What kind of cookies?

How long till they're ready?

Can I have three?

WHAT MOM CREATED WHEN SHE USED HER NEW MIXER.

Now arrange the circled letters to form the surprise answer, as suggested by the above cartoon.

Print answer here

A

JUMBLE®

Unscramble these four Jumbles, one letter to each square, to form four ordinary words.

SIONE

DUGIE

PAPNYS

GORNTS

Welcome   On the house

PFSSST

WHAT THE CUS-
TOMER EXPERI-
ENCED WHEN HE
VISITED THE
NEW PUB.

Now arrange the circled letters to form the surprise answer, as suggested by the above cartoon.

Print answer here   A ⃝⃝⃝⃝⃝ " ⃝⃝⃝⃝⃝⃝⃝ "

JUMBLE®

Unscramble these four Jumbles, one letter to
each square, to form four ordinary words.

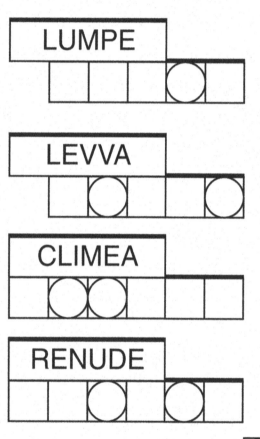

LUMPE

LEVVA

CLIMEA

RENUDE

What's wrong --
You OK?

Going
fishing

WHEN HE WAS
AWAKENED EARLY,
HIS WIFE WAS ---

Now arrange the circled letters to form the
surprise answer, as suggested by the above
cartoon.

Print answer here

JUMBLE®

Unscramble these four Jumbles, one letter to each square, to form four ordinary words.

SLARN

SEPIO

THOTEG

LARNAC

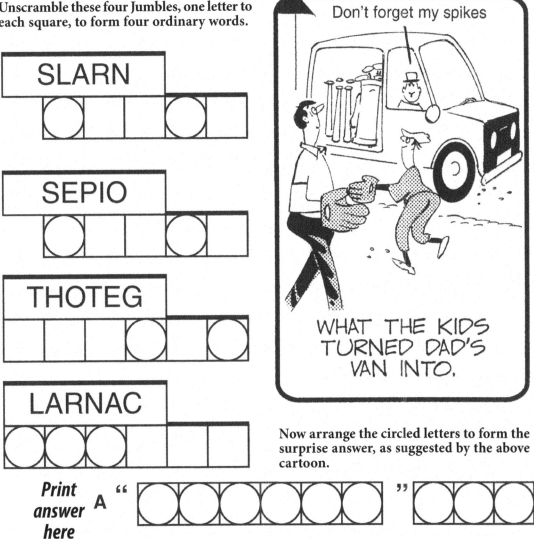

Don't forget my spikes

WHAT THE KIDS
TURNED DAD'S
VAN INTO.

Now arrange the circled letters to form the surprise answer, as suggested by the above cartoon.

Print
answer
here

A " ⬡⬡⬡⬡⬡⬡ " ⬡⬡⬡

JUMBLE®

Unscramble these four Jumbles, one letter to
each square, to form four ordinary words.

BLAWR

WULFA

EMBURP

CEDITE

She's very
protective

They're
beautiful

HOW THE LIONESS
FELT WHEN SUR-
ROUNDED BY
HER CUBS.

Now arrange the circled letters to form the
surprise answer, as suggested by the above
cartoon.

*Print
answer
here*

OF " "

JUMBLE®

Unscramble these four Jumbles, one letter to each square, to form four ordinary words.

AXORB

USSEO

EXFRIP

BIDITT

For me? I'll always wear it

WHAT SHE DID WHEN SHE RE-CEIVED A NECK-LACE FROM THE PIRATE CHEST.

Now arrange the circled letters to form the surprise answer, as suggested by the above cartoon.

Print answer here " ☐☐☐☐☐☐☐☐☐ " ☐☐

JUMBLE®

Unscramble these four Jumbles, one letter to each square, to form four ordinary words.

FYNAC

LOHLE

RAYSOV

MABGIT

It's so noisy in here   Everyone's gabbing

WHAT THE COM-PUTER STAFF CONSIDERED THE BREAK LOUNGE.

Now arrange the circled letters to form the surprise answer, as suggested by the above cartoon.

Print answer here A

JUMBLE®

Unscramble these four Jumbles, one letter to each square, to form four ordinary words.

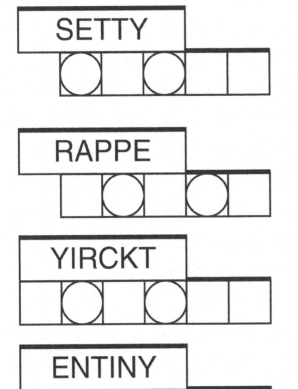

SETTY

RAPPE

YIRCKT

ENTINY

Uh, oh -- she's not laughing

WHAT SHE GAVE HIM AFTER HER SPILL AT THE SKATING RINK.

Now arrange the circled letters to form the surprise answer, as suggested by the above cartoon.

Print answer here   AN " ⬡⬡⬡ " ⬡⬡⬡⬡⬡

JUMBLE®

Unscramble these four Jumbles, one letter to each square, to form four ordinary words.

TIHHC

IDDEA

TEETIP

SOUREA

The Giants will run over them

No way

Barkeep, another one

A CONVERSATION AT A SPORTS BAR CAN BECOME THIS.

Now arrange the circled letters to form the surprise answer, as suggested by the above cartoon.

Print answer here " ◯◯◯◯◯◯◯◯ "

JUMBLE®

Unscramble these four Jumbles, one letter to each square, to form four ordinary words.

PLOIT

MYPTE

AVEGAS

TAISER

You're late. No dinner tonight

WHY JUNIOR DIDN'T GET ANY SUPPER.

Now arrange the circled letters to form the surprise answer, as suggested by the above cartoon.

Print answer here   IT WAS

JUMBLE®

Unscramble these four Jumbles, one letter to each square, to form four ordinary words.

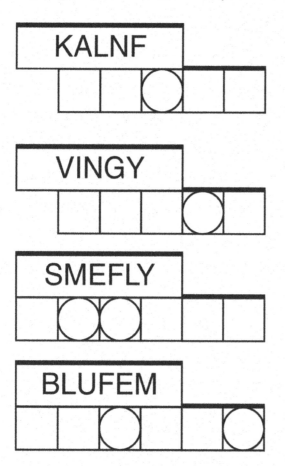

KALNF

VINGY

SMEFLY

BLUFEM

Did you do your homework, make your lunch, clean your---

Yup yup yup

WHAT THE TEEN TURNED INTO WHEN MOM ASKED THE QUESTIONS.

Now arrange the circled letters to form the surprise answer, as suggested by the above cartoon.

Print answer here A " ◯◯◯ " ◯◯◯

JUMBLE®

Unscramble these four Jumbles, one letter to
each square, to form four ordinary words.

KIHCC

CUTOS

INJEYT

GAROUC

I challenge
you

Take it to
the magistrate

WHERE MEDIEVAL
DISPUTES WERE
OFTEN SETTLED.

Now arrange the circled letters to form the
surprise answer, as suggested by the above
cartoon.

Print answer
here   IN

JUMBLE

Unscramble these four Jumbles, one letter to each square, to form four ordinary words.

HASAB

ZAMIE

DORVOE

RULBET

We're making a fortune

WHEN THE BOYS CLEARED DRIVEWAYS AFTER THE STORM THEY---

Now arrange the circled letters to form the surprise answer, as suggested by the above cartoon.

Print answer here

⬡⬡⬡⬡⬡⬡⬡⬡⬡ ⬡⬡ IN

JUMBLE®

Unscramble these four Jumbles, one letter to
each square, to form four ordinary words.

KECHE

OXMAI

CROTAF

LORCAR

I'm scalped!

They're butchers

WHAT THE BARBERS
WERE KNOWN AS
AT THE BASE.

Now arrange the circled letters to form the
surprise answer, as suggested by the above
cartoon.

**Print
answer** THE
here

157

JUMBLE®

Unscramble these four Jumbles, one letter to
each square, to form four ordinary words.

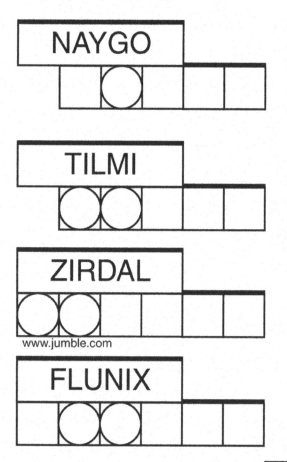

NAYGO

TILMI

ZIRDAL

www.jumble.com

FLUNIX

This is excellent

WHEN THE DENTIST
MADE A PIE, HE
EXCELLED AT THIS,
NATURALLY.

Now arrange the circled letters to form the
surprise answer, as suggested by the above
cartoon.

Print answer here THE

158

JUMBLE®

Unscramble these four Jumbles, one letter to each square, to form four ordinary words.

MONGE

OATAR

BILBEN

CUIMPE

WHAT THE FISHER-MAN WANTED TO INCREASE.

Now arrange the circled letters to form the surprise answer, as suggested by the above cartoon.

Print answer here HIS " ◯◯◯ " ◯◯◯◯◯◯

JUMBLE®

Unscramble these four Jumbles, one letter to each square, to form four ordinary words.

GUNST

DOORE

HAPNOR

LAPLID

.I didn't sleep a wink

HOW HE FELT WHEN FIDO BARKED ALL NIGHT.

Now arrange the circled letters to form the surprise answer, as suggested by the above cartoon.

Print answer here

JUMBLE®

Unscramble these four Jumbles, one letter to each square, to form four ordinary words.

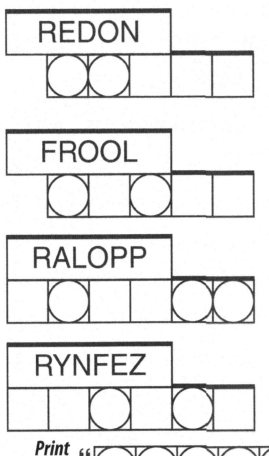

REDON

FROOL

RALOPP

RYNFEZ

That's it! I'm taking it down and starting over

Calm down

WHAT HE DID WHEN HE COULDN'T FIX THE CEILING LEAK.

Now arrange the circled letters to form the surprise answer, as suggested by the above cartoon.

Print answer here " ⟨⟩⟨⟩⟨⟩⟨⟩⟨⟩ " THE ⟨⟩⟨⟩⟨⟩⟨⟩

JUMBLE®

Unscramble these four Jumbles, one letter to each square, to form four ordinary words.

BRUTS

GAREW

INNACE

REMMEB

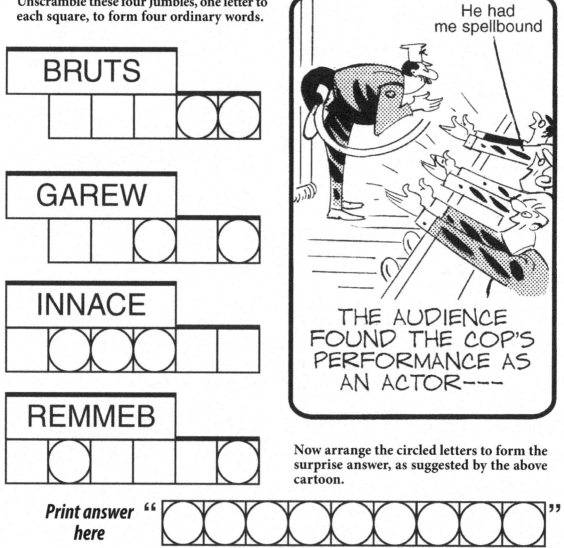

He had me spellbound

THE AUDIENCE FOUND THE COP'S PERFORMANCE AS AN ACTOR---

Now arrange the circled letters to form the surprise answer, as suggested by the above cartoon.

Print answer here "◯◯◯◯◯◯◯◯◯◯"

Ready, Set,

JUMBLE®

Challenger Puzzles

JUMBLE

Unscramble these six Jumbles, one letter to
each square, to form six ordinary words.

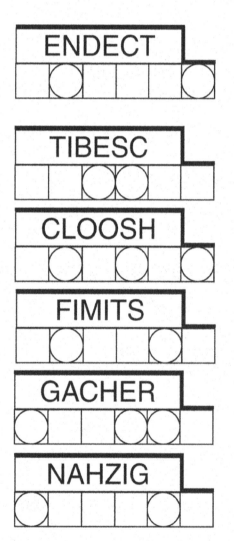

ENDECT

TIBESC

CLOOSH

FIMITS

GACHER

NAHZIG

Oh, just what we need.
No more plastic forks

WHEN THE COUPLE
GOT SILVERWARE AS
A WEDDING GIFT,
THEY SAID IT WAS A——

Now arrange the circled letters to form the
surprise answer, as suggested by the above
cartoon.

Print answer here

“ ”

JUMBLE®

Unscramble these six Jumbles, one letter to each square, to form six ordinary words.

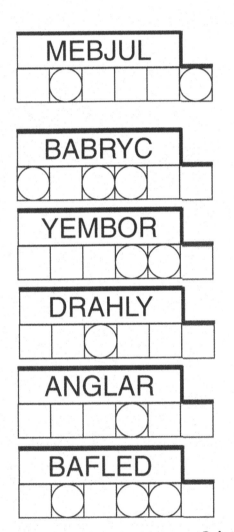

MEBJUL

BABRYC

YEMBOR

DRAHLY

ANGLAR

BAFLED

This section holds my vintage collection

TO SUCCEED, THE WINE MERCHANT NEEDED A – – –

Now arrange the circled letters to form the surprise answer, as suggested by the above cartoon.

Print answer here

⬡⬡⬡⬡⬡ AND ⬡ " ⬡⬡⬡⬡⬡⬡ "

JUMBLE®

Unscramble these six Jumbles, one letter to
each square, to form six ordinary words.

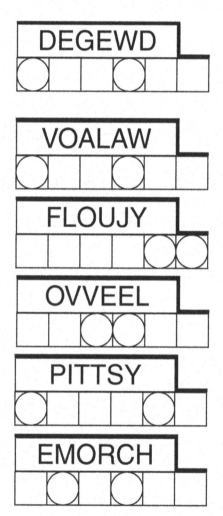

DEGEWD

VOALAW

FLOUJY

OVVEEL

PITTSY

EMORCH

Wow, I should have looked
at the prices

WHEN THE CHECK
CAME FOR HIS
JUICY, TENDER
STEAK, IT WAS——

Now arrange the circled letters to form the
surprise answer, as suggested by the above
cartoon.

Print answer here

⬡⬡⬡⬡⬡ TO ⬡⬡⬡⬡⬡⬡⬡

JUMBLE®

Unscramble these six Jumbles, one letter to each square, to form six ordinary words.

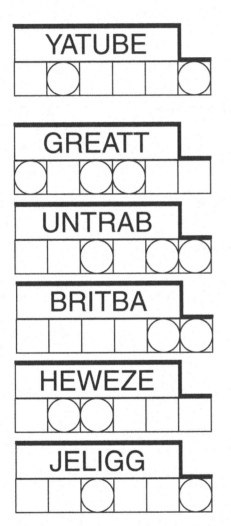

YATUBE

GREATT

UNTRAB

BRITBA

HEWEZE

JELIGG

Well! Well! And how are we this morning?

DURING ROUNDS, THE CARDIOLOGIST GAVE HIS PATIENT A---

Now arrange the circled letters to form the surprise answer, as suggested by the above cartoon.

Print answer here

167

PUZZLE
165

JUMBLE®

Unscramble these six Jumbles, one letter to
each square, to form six ordinary words.

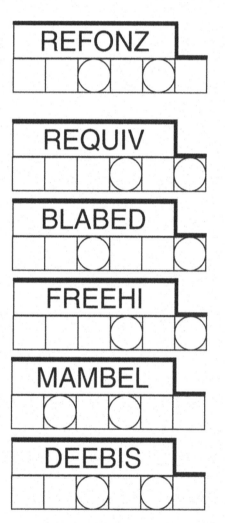

REFONZ

REQUIV

BLABED

FREEHI

MAMBEL

DEEBIS

He used to be awful

Yeah,
now
he's
terrible

WHERE THE POET
ENDED UP GOING
DURING THE
COURSE OF HIS
CAREER.

Now arrange the circled letters to form the
surprise answer, as suggested by the above
cartoon.

Print answer here

TO "

168

JUMBLE®

Unscramble these six Jumbles, one letter to each square, to form six ordinary words.

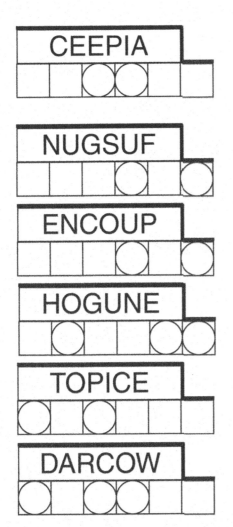

CEEPIA

NUGSUF

ENCOUP

HOGUNE

TOPICE

DARCOW

I'll do the dishes next ——— He must want the car tonight

WHEN JUNIOR VOL- UNTEERED TO CLEAN THE HOUSE, MOM SAID IT WAS A---

Now arrange the circled letters to form the surprise answer, as suggested by the above cartoon.

Print answer here

" ☐☐☐☐☐☐☐☐ " ☐☐☐☐☐☐

JUMBLE®

Unscramble these six Jumbles, one letter to
each square, to form six ordinary words.

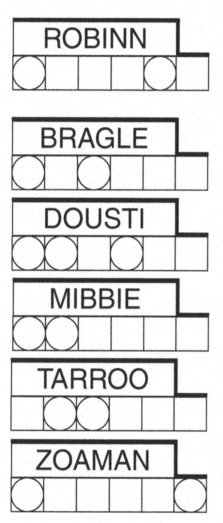

ROBINN

BRAGLE

DOUSTI

MIBBIE

TARROO

ZOAMAN

Mix until it's as smooth
as a caress

He's such
a ham

THE TV CHEF
TURNED THE
COOKING SHOW
INTO THIS.

Now arrange the circled letters to form the
surprise answer, as suggested by the above
cartoon.

Print answer here

A "⬡⬡⬡⬡⬡⬡⬡⬡" ⬡⬡⬡⬡⬡

170

JUMBLE®

Unscramble these six Jumbles, one letter to
each square, to form six ordinary words.

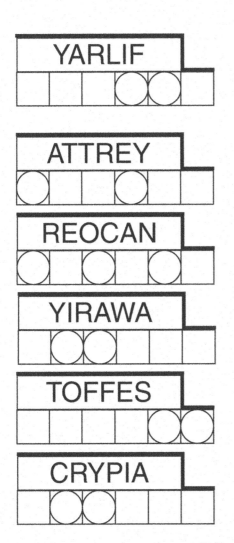

YARLIF

ATTREY

REOCAN

YIRAWA

TOFFES

CRYPIA

She's a good
mother

WHAT THE MAIL-
MAN'S DOG TURNED
INTO WHEN SHE
HAD PUPPIES.

Now arrange the circled letters to form the
surprise answer, as suggested by the above
cartoon.

Print answer here

A

171

JUMBLE®

Unscramble these six Jumbles, one letter to
each square, to form six ordinary words.

SELUNS

LAISOC

REBAWE

SHEERY

PARMEE

DEGAAM

Make sure
the lights
are low

DIRECTOR

AVOIDED BY THE
EXOTIC DANCER.

Now arrange the circled letters to form the
surprise answer, as suggested by the above
cartoon.

Print answer here

A " ◯◯◯◯◯ " ◯◯◯◯◯◯◯◯◯

JUMBLE®

Unscramble these six Jumbles, one letter to each square, to form six ordinary words.

MAROFT

REALOP

FORFET

PINGRY

SLEENT

WUSBAY

So much for Sunday in the park

Sunny all day

WHAT THE SUDDEN RAIN DID TO THE PICNICKERS.

Now arrange the circled letters to form the surprise answer, as suggested by the above cartoon.

Print answer here

" ◯◯◯ " THEIR ◯◯◯◯◯◯◯◯◯

JUMBLE®

Unscramble these six Jumbles, one letter to
each square, to form six ordinary words.

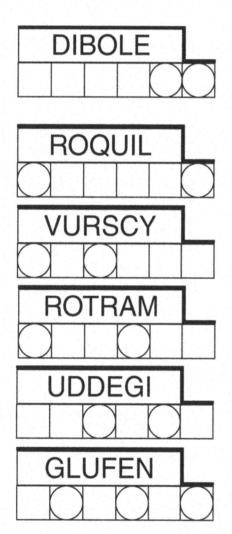

DIBOLE

ROQUIL

VURSCY

ROTRAM

UDDEGI

GLUFEN

I've got a tip
on number 5

So do I

THEY BET ON
THE SAME HORSE
BECAUSE THEY
WERE---

Now arrange the circled letters to form the
surprise answer, as suggested by the above
cartoon.

Print answer here

PUZZLE
172

JUMBLE.

Unscramble these six Jumbles, one letter to
each square, to form six ordinary words.

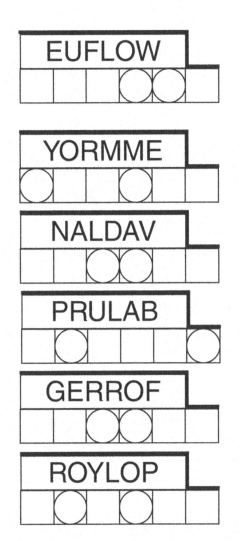

EUFLOW

YORMME

NALDAV

PRULAB

GERROF

ROYLOP

Do a good job and soon
you'll be cutting steaks

HOW THE BUTCHER
GOT AHEAD IN
HIS JOB.

Now arrange the circled letters to form the
surprise answer, as suggested by the above
cartoon.

Print answer here

THE "   "

175

JUMBLE®

Unscramble these six Jumbles, one letter to each square, to form six ordinary words.

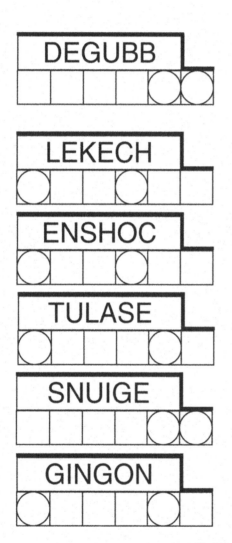

DEGUBB

LEKECH

ENSHOC

TULASE

SNUIGE

GINGON

I'll give you $250

Sorry, that's the price

$300

WHAT THE SHOP OWNER DID WHEN THE HUNTER MADE HIM AN OFFER.

Now arrange the circled letters to form the surprise answer, as suggested by the above cartoon.

Print answer here

TO

176

JUMBLE®

Unscramble these six Jumbles, one letter to
each square, to form six ordinary words.

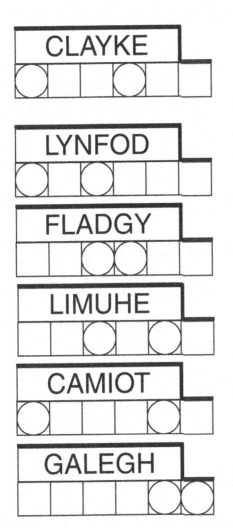

CLAYKE

LYNFOD

FLADGY

LIMUHE

CAMIOT

GALEGH

By the way, Harold,
my fur coat is
getting a bit
shabby

Oh, my aching
back

WHY SHE GAVE
HER HUSBAND
A MASSAGE.

Now arrange the circled letters to form the
surprise answer, as suggested by the above
cartoon.

Print answer here

TO ⬡⬡⬡⬡⬡⬡⬡ A "⬡⬡⬡⬡⬡"

JUMBLE®

Unscramble these six Jumbles, one letter to
each square, to form six ordinary words.

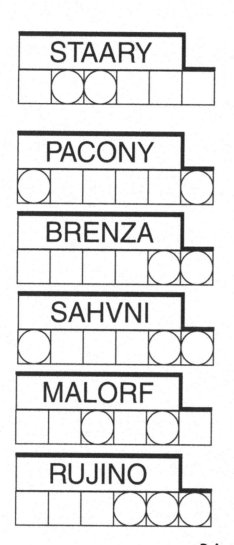

STAARY

PACONY

BRENZA

SAHVNI

MALORF

RUJINO

He's close to the wire

WHAT THE SULKY
DRIVER WANTED TO
DO WHEN HE
LED THE RACE.

Now arrange the circled letters to form the
surprise answer, as suggested by the above
cartoon.

Print answer here

" ◯◯◯◯◯◯◯ " ◯◯◯◯◯◯◯◯

PUZZLE
176

JUMBLE®

Unscramble these six Jumbles, one letter to each square, to form six ordinary words.

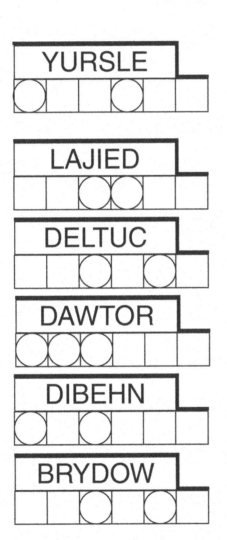

YURSLE

LAJIED

DELTUC

DAWTOR

DIBEHN

BRYDOW

WHAT THE REFEREE BECAME WHEN THE TEAMS GOT UNRULY.

Now arrange the circled letters to form the surprise answer, as suggested by the above cartoon.

Print answer here

A ⬡⬡⬡⬡⬡⬡⬡ - ⬡⬡⬡⬡⬡⬡

179

JUMBLE®

Unscramble these six Jumbles, one letter to each square, to form six ordinary words.

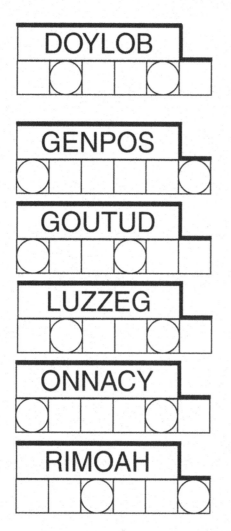

DOYLOB

GENPOS

GOUTUD

LUZZEG

ONNACY

RIMOAH

Why isn't this roast warm?

It WAS-- two hours ago

WHEN THE BUTCHER WAS LATE FOR DINNER, HIS WIFE GAVE HIM THIS.

Now arrange the circled letters to form the surprise answer, as suggested by the above cartoon.

Print answer here

THE ⬡⬡⬡⬡ " ⬡⬡⬡⬡⬡⬡⬡ "

JUMBLE®

Unscramble these six Jumbles, one letter to each square, to form six ordinary words.

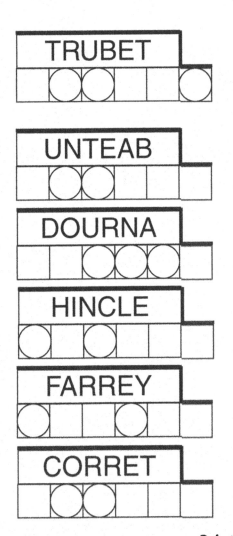

TRUBET

UNTEAB

DOURNA

HINCLE

FARREY

CORRET

We've become best friends

We share our problems

THE SOCIOLOGIST JOINED THE REG-ULARS AT THE COFFEE SHOP TO STUDY THE---

Now arrange the circled letters to form the surprise answer, as suggested by the above cartoon.

Print answer here

" ◯◯◯◯◯◯◯ " ◯◯◯◯◯◯

181

JUMBLE®

Unscramble these six Jumbles, one letter to each square, to form six ordinary words.

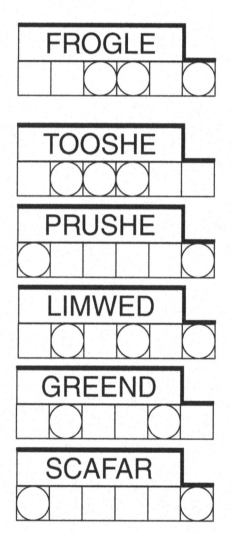

FROGLE

TOOSHE

PRUSHE

LIMWED

GREEND

SCAFAR

THIS HAPPENED WHEN THE NURSERY'S SALES INCREASED.

Now arrange the circled letters to form the surprise answer, as suggested by the above cartoon.

Print answer here

JUMBLE®

Unscramble these six Jumbles, one letter to each square, to form six ordinary words.

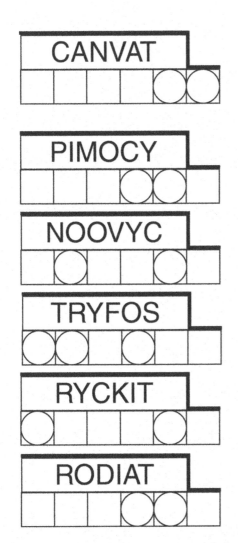

CANVAT

PIMOCY

NOOVYC

TRYFOS

RYCKIT

RODIAT

Dig the sound of that CD player

WHAT THE DISC JOCKEY DID WITH HIS NEW CAR.

Now arrange the circled letters to form the surprise answer, as suggested by the above cartoon.

Print answer here

○○○○ ○○ ○○○ A "○○○○"

183

Answers

1. **Jumbles:** TEMPO SHEEP THEORY BOTTLE
   Answer: What all those suggestions about improving the doughnut business seemed to have—HOLES IN THEM

2. **Jumbles:** FOCUS BALKY TORRID LEEWAY
   Answer: What a hyphen permits you to do—BREAK YOUR WORD

3. **Jumbles:** POISE ADAPT EMBRYO DEFILE
   Answer: How a stag is often forced to run—FOR "DEER" LIFE

4. **Jumbles:** AZURE BERET WALRUS ORIGIN
   Answer: Some people might rise higher if they'd learn to do this—RISE EARLIER

5. **Jumbles:** CABIN LITHE GOSPEL HELPER
   Answer: One isn't sure to say it—PERHAPS

6. **Jumbles:** FRAME SOAPY QUEASY CHROME
   Answer: "Did you hear my last joke?"—"I SURE HOPE SO"

7. **Jumbles:** UNWED BOOTH EGOISM PEOPLE
   Answer: What a guy who acts like a heel should be—STEPPED ON

8. **Jumbles:** AMITY WRATH DENOTE SECOND
   Answer: What those young history teachers did at their annual get-together—MADE "DATES"

9. **Jumbles:** TYING CHAOS BEATEN WOBBLE
   Answer: How people saw things after the discovery of electricity—IN A NEW LIGHT

10. **Jumbles:** MESSY PURGE CRABBY HAPPEN
    Answer: What flatfeet can be—THE "ARCH ENEMY"

11. **Jumbles:** TRULY SWOON PUDDLE RACIAL
    Answer: What the Earth's two polar regions are—A WORLD APART

12. **Jumbles:** WALTZ COLON MOROSE STUDIO
    Answer: Who saw the dinosaur entering the restaurant?—THE DINERS SAW

13. **Jumbles:** HABIT VISOR SCENIC PARODY
    Answer: There's a close relationship between a man's position and this—HIS DISPOSITION

14. **Jumbles:** OWING LOGIC POPLAR CLEAVE
    Answer: Meant the disappearance of the carriage—THE "CAR AGE"

15. **Jumbles:** CHAFF DICED GLOBAL JUNIOR
    Answer: A stick-in-the-mud found in a ship—THE ANCHOR

16. **Jumbles:** WEDGE BASIS PUMICE QUARTZ
    Answer: What tantrums are for some kids these days—QUITE THE RAGE

17. **Jumbles:** OCCUR STOOP PODIUM HYBRID
    Answer: When it comes to love, an engagement ring is this—A "BUY" PRODUCT

18. **Jumbles:** CLEFT OAKEN FINISH INFUSE
    Answer: It was off-season for fishing, which is why the sheriff made it this—"OFF-FISH-AL" (official)

19. **Jumbles:** DERBY CRAWL BEAVER LAYMAN
    Answer: What the bank robber got when the security system sounded—"ALARMED"

20. **Jumbles:** EAGLE FAIRY LANCER POPLAR
    Answer: What to do when the barometer falls—REPLACE THE NAIL

21. **Jumbles:** CREEK ALBUM SHERRY MIDWAY
    Answer: What the beekeeper said on an unusually hot day—IT'S "SWARM" HERE

22. **Jumbles:** STEED HARPY WHENCE BEFOUL
    Answer: What the sign on the door of opportunity reads—"PUSH"

23. **Jumbles:** GAILY SWISH GRAVEN CALIPH
    Answer: They resided on the roof because they loved this—"HIGH LIVING"

24. **Jumbles:** SWAMP ENEMY CHALET PONCHO
    Answer: "There's a strange drip in the basement. Shall I call the plumber?"—"NO, THE COPS"

25. **Jumbles:** PRIZE DRONE SCARCE DAMASK
    Answer: A person of good judgment knows when to speak his mind and when to do this—MIND HOW HE SPEAKS

26. **Jumbles:** BAKED CANAL PODIUM NOGGIN
    Answer: What the job of delivering parcels sometimes is—A BANG-UP ONE

27. **Jumbles:** WHISK COUGH GENTRY UNHOOK
    Answer: In order to please his wife, he reluctantly agreed to go there—OUT OF HIS "WEIGH"

28. **Jumbles:** HIKER MADLY CANKER BABIED
    Answer: The acrobat was the only guy who knew how to talk about himself—BEHIND HIS OWN BACK

29. **Jumbles:** SCARY FRIAR BLUISH RAVAGE
    Answer: What came between those two poets turned professional boxers?—"VERSUS" (verses)

30. **Jumbles:** QUIRE AGONY DEADLY ENGINE
    Answer: What kind of an experience is it to travel by flying carpet?—A RUGGED ONE

31. **Jumbles:** JOUST HENNA MALTED BUTTON
    Answer: That blonde sure has something that'll knock your eye out—A HUSBAND

32. **Jumbles:** HENCE UNITY JUNKET SHAKEN
    Answer: In the pen doing a long sentence—THE INK

33. **Jumbles:** BEGUN VOCAL EMPIRE MAYHEM
    Answer: Could this beer be large?—"LAGER"

34. **Jumbles:** SYLPH COUPE RADIUS TANGLE
    Answer: What those old-time veterinarians used to make—"HORSE" CALLS

35. **Jumbles:** ADMIT CAKED FAULTY PLACID
    Answer: A careful driver is the guy who has just seen the car in front of him get this—A TICKET

36. **Jumbles:** ODDLY TOKEN CONVEX INLAID
    Answer: Why the jury asked to see the accused safecracker again—THEY WERE DEAD "LOCKED"

37. **Jumbles:** RUMMY MONEY GIBBET HUNTER
    Answer: What might Tom do when his car breaks down?—TOM "THUMB"

38. **Jumbles:** TOOTH DIZZY BOBBIN ICEBOX
    Answer: An "addiction" to this can cause some people to become sleepy—"DICTION"

39. **Jumbles:** MESSY VIRUS HOOKED SCRIBE
    Answer: What that amorous pitcher knew how to throw best—KISSES

40. **Jumbles:** FENCE PRIME GOATEE NOODLE
    Answer: What might go on inside a compass?—"NEEDLE POINT"

41. **Jumbles:** WOVEN BLIMP EFFORT POORLY
    Answer: What are you when you have something on the boss?—"FIRE PROOF"

42. **Jumbles:** ELUDE QUAKE STUPID IMPOSE
    Answer: What the garbage man said he was—"AT HER DISPOSAL"

43. **Jumbles:** MIRTH SWISH HEIFER BIGAMY
    Answer: How to find out if your watch is gaining—WEIGH IT

44. **Jumbles:** ELITE FELON TRYING LAUNCH
    Answer: When he finally got the fireplace working, she was this—"GRATE-FULL"

45. **Jumbles:** BATHE HIKER SMUDGE POROUS
    Answer: When the cowboys finished branding them, the cows were really this—"IMPRESSED"

46. **Jumbles:** GLADE JUDGE BEWAIL INTACT
    Answer: What the workers did to get a pay raise—"WAGED" A BATTLE

47. **Jumbles:** AGILE HEAVY BANDIT FABRIC
    Answer: A long word that doesn't mean a lot—ABBREVIATED

184

48. **Jumbles:** UNITY PIETY TARTAR POORLY
Answer: The sales manager favored a window of—
OPPORTUNITY

49. **Jumbles:** FRAUD SHEAF PRYING INWARD
Answer: How they kept the mummy at the secret dig—
"UNDER WRAPS"

50. **Jumbles:** UNCLE BULGY RARITY CANYON
Answer: What the overworked cook experienced—
"BURN" OUT

51. **Jumbles:** KNELL TRYST FOURTH MIDWAY
Answer: Tough for a night watchman to avoid stealing—
FORTY WINKS

52. **Jumbles:** DOWNY ANKLE ACTING OUTING
Answer: Moms were doing this years before computerized living—GOING ON LINE

53. **Jumbles:** STOOP ENTRY MATRON FIGURE
Answer: Reciting a verse can turn a morning run into this—
POETRY IN MOTION

54. **Jumbles:** LIMBO JULEP FONDLY BROOCH
Answer: The winning driver turned his victory lap into this—A "JOY" RIDE

55. **Jumbles:** YACHT DECRY JUSTLY FRIEZE
Answer: Why the medical student liked ham—
IT'S EASILY "CURED"

56. **Jumbles:** TRIPE ELDER RENDER RAREFY
Answer: The saucy actress' fans thought she was—
REEL "PERT-Y"

57. **Jumbles:** BISON BALMY JESTER CHOSEN
Answer: The brass band turned the traffic tie-up into this—
A "JAM" SESSION

58. **Jumbles:** GORGE ELITE LATEST BURLAP
Answer: What he hoped the movie would turn into—
A REAL "SLEEPER"

59. **Jumbles:** OUTDO FEVER METRIC PARITY
Answer: Easy to lose with a rowdy class—YOUR TEMPER

60. **Jumbles:** CRACK AGING ENJOIN GOVERN
Answer: What he considered his nearly bankrupt business—
A "GOING" CONCERN

61. **Jumbles:** POACH ABIDE GASKET BUTANE
Answer: Where the boxer ended up when he started losing—ON THE "BEATEN" PATH

62. **Jumbles:** GULLY RAINY LADING CABANA
Answer: What it takes to be an Army bugler—A "CALLING"

63. **Jumbles:** TULLE COVEY PAYING IMPEND
Answer: He avoided the fancy barbershop because he didn't want to—GET CLIPPED

64. **Jumbles:** FACET NUDGE STUDIO SCHEME
Answer: What it took for the boarder to finish dinner—
"SECONDS"

65. **Jumbles:** ENACT INEPT CLOUDY DUGOUT
Answer: Why the butcher was fired—HE COULDN'T "CUT" IT

66. **Jumbles:** CHAIR GASSY INVOKE BANGLE
Answer: Why did the patrons frequent the happy hour?—
FOR "BAR-GAINS"

67. **Jumbles:** BOWER REARM BUOYED FIRING
Answer: What the young electrician did when he was broke—"WIRED" FOR MONEY

68. **Jumbles:** RUMMY TRULY HICCUP SUBTLY
Answer: An art student will do this before an exam—
BRUSH UP

69. **Jumbles:** EXTOL NEWLY SEAMAN ELICIT
Answer: What the store owner gave the ladder buyer—
AN EXTENSION

70. **Jumbles:** DOUBT WHEEL POISON VESTRY
Answer: Where the waiter landed when he dropped the tureen—IN THE SOUP

71. **Jumbles:** HONOR SCARY ALIGHT MUFFLE
Answer: What the charter pilot considered the planeload of society matrons—A FLIGHT OF "FANCY"

72. **Jumbles:** BEFIT BROOK TERROR TURTLE
Answer: He won the poker hand because he was—
A BETTER BETTOR

73. **Jumbles:** BRAND GUEST FRIGID LAYOFF
Answer: What she considered his high-speed exit from the freeway—A "TURN OFF"

74. **Jumbles:** GUILD ROACH ANYHOW JIGGER
Answer: How the art contest ended up—IN A "DRAW"

75. **Jumbles:** IDIOT TOOTH FORKED CRAVAT
Answer: What the CEO did when the loan was approved—
TOOK THE "CREDIT"

76. **Jumbles:** ADULT FOYER PROFIT POETIC
Answer: Important to wear to her wedding—
THE "RITE" OUTFIT

77. **Jumbles:** RHYME TITLE BABIED GENDER
Answer: What the nurse did when she gave the body-builder a shot—SHE "NEEDLED" HIM

78. **Jumbles:** YOKEL COLON HIDING GENIUS
Answer: What she did before going on line on a cold night—
"LOGGED" ON

79. **Jumbles:** TEPID BANAL TANKER DULCET
Answer: Easy to do these days with a ten dollar bill—
BREAK IT

80. **Jumbles:** APART LYRIC AROUND PONCHO
Answer: Despite the noise, easy to hear in a bowling alley—
A PIN DROP

81. **Jumbles:** LYING TOXIC INHALE SURELY
Answer: Changing muffler and tailpipe can be this—
"EXHAUSTING"

82. **Jumbles:** WHEAT FLAME ADMIRE SALUTE
Answer: Buying a cheap watch can turn out to be—
A WASTE OF "TIME"

83. **Jumbles:** TABOO TEMPO UNHOOK JAILED
Answer: Selling prunes turned out to be this—A "PLUM" JOB

84. **Jumbles:** DINER FENCE BARIUM WEAKEN
Answer: What she turned into when her loaf of rye won the blue ribbon—THE BREAD WINNER

85. **Jumbles:** WEIGH TARRY RADIUS GADFLY
Answer: Studying for a difficult nutrition exam can be—
HARD TO "DIGEST"

86. **Jumbles:** FOCUS CRUSH BLEACH ASTRAY
Answer: You might call that fine student drama this—
A "CLASS" ACT

87. **Jumbles:** MERGE IMBUE DISOWN MAYHEM
Answer: What the busboy received from his maximum effort—A MINIMUM WAGE

88. **Jumbles:** CARGO FABLE BOUGHT JOCUND
Answer: He carefully fixed the boss's transmission because it was—A "CLUTCH" JOB

89. **Jumbles:** KNOWN BOUND SPEEDY FAMOUS
Answer: The elevator operator wasn't bothered by this at the stock exchange—UPS AND DOWNS

90. **Jumbles:** ROUSE EJECT DEFINE FIESTA
Answer: What the halfback experienced after the crushing tackle—"SIDE" EFFECTS

91. **Jumbles:** ARDOR BRINY LEEWAY TUMULT
Answer: Why did the crooked cleaner take the money to the bank?—TO "LAUNDER" IT

92. **Jumbles:** FETID CABLE CASKET DONKEY
Answer: What the group did on the bridge cruise—
STACKED THE DECK

93. **Jumbles:** CAPON HOIST ADROIT PITIED
Answer: Where the squabbling kids drove Dad—
TO DISTRACTION

94. **Jumbles:** ITCHY LILAC MYSTIC RANCOR
Answer: What he said when he made a belt in craft class—
IT'S A "CINCH"

95. **Jumbles:** USURY AFOOT BUTTER CONVOY
Answer: When the prizefighter became a census taker he was—OUT FOR THE COUNT

96. **Jumbles:** BEGOT CYNIC TOTTER MOHAIR
Answer: What he brought home when he took the pigs to market—THE BACON

97. **Jumbles:** GLOAT VILLA MUFFIN FAULTY
Answer: A tough jigsaw puzzle can lead to this—A FIT FIT

98. **Jumbles:** VIGIL ACRID BLOODY CAUCUS
Answer: What the hippies considered the igloo—"COOL" DIGS

99. **Jumbles:** MERCY CLOAK DROWSY SINFUL
Answer: A good photographer will do this—"FOCUS" ON HIS WORK

100. **Jumbles:** LINER TRILL WATERY LACING
Answer: What the monitor turned into when the students broke the rules—THE LAWN RANGER

101. **Jumbles:** RAVEN ELUDE ENTAIL RECTOR
Answer: What the grocer gave her when the fruit spoiled—A ROTTEN DEAL

102. **Jumbles:** KITTY ICILY FLAXEN QUEASY
Answer: What was needed when the old buggy finally broke down—A QUICK FIX

103. **Jumbles:** PHOTO OXIDE EIGHTY GROUCH
Answer: What the mountain climbers paid to reach the summit—A "HIGH" PRICE

104. **Jumbles:** SANDY YODEL WEDGED COWARD
Answer: Why the bookies fought—THEY WERE AT "ODDS"

105. **Jumbles:** UNWED LIGHT MAINLY MARVEL
Answer: What the photographer ended up with when he made a pass—A NEGATIVE

106. **Jumbles:** GOUGE CRAZE AMBUSH MORBID
Answer: To the ball players, the conductor's music stand was this—A "SCORE" BOARD

107. **Jumbles:** SORRY DUCHY HECKLE FIZZLE
Answer: Easy to do at a junkyard—"RE-CYCLE"

108. **Jumbles:** DOILY AVAIL NEARLY CUDDLE
Answer: What he did after working around the clock—CALLED IT A "DAY"

109. **Jumbles:** DANDY WIPED DOOMED BLOUSE
Answer: Where they ended up when the nearby property became a landfill—DOWN IN THE "DUMPS"

110. **Jumbles:** HEDGE HAIRY SOOTHE HECTIC
Answer: He listened to his favorite song when doing his gardening—"HI HOE, HI HOE"

111. **Jumbles:** LITHE FAMED ABDUCT SCORCH
Answer: What Mom made Junior do when he tried to duck piano practice—FACE THE MUSIC

112. **Jumbles:** FEWER SKULK CASHEW OSSIFY
Answer: A good way to receive a safe driving award—BE WRECK-LESS

113. **Jumbles:** BRAVO CABIN JAUNTY DELUXE
Answer: What he got when he disobeyed Mom at the beach—TANNED

114. **Jumbles:** EMERY SAUTE PUSHER CUDGEL
Answer: Cutting down those beautiful trees left them like this—"STUMPED"

115. **Jumbles:** STOKE BRASS UTMOST CENSUS
Answer: The medical students said their final exams were—"STRESS" TESTS

116. **Jumbles:** PRINT TUNED IODINE BEFOUL
Answer: Why the depressed businessman took the elevator—HE NEEDED A "LIFT"

117. **Jumbles:** NAÏVE ROBIN TONGUE GIGOLO
Answer: Making vases was his way of doing this—"URNING" A LIVING

118. **Jumbles:** BROOD COCOA PONDER MOBILE
Answer: What a salesman gets when he's on the road—ROOM AND BORED

119. **Jumbles:** CUBIC RAPID PAGODA HYBRID
Answer: When he splashed her at the pool party, she thought he was—A BIG DRIP

120. **Jumbles:** POWER YOUTH FERVOR GOLFER
Answer: What the conductor told the obnoxious passengers—WHERE TO GET OFF

121. **Jumbles:** OLDER GUISE ASTHMA INVERT
Answer: What he made when he began running to get fit—GREAT STRIDES

122. **Jumbles:** TARDY INLET FRUGAL SLEEPY
Answer: The pub owner threw out the statue because it was—"PLASTERED"

123. **Jumbles:** WHILE TAKEN TOWARD STIGMA
Answer: What happened to the bodybuilder's shape when he gained weight—IT WENT TO WAIST

124. **Jumbles:** COUGH FAITH STUCCO CLUMSY
Answer: What he wanted on his hot dog—HIS MOUTH

125. **Jumbles:** TWINE PANSY SINGLE CHERUB
Answer: Tough for some to sleep without this—A NIGHTCAP

126. **Jumbles:** HAVOC BUSHY PLURAL EFFACE
Answer: What the house painter got when his bid was too high—THE "BRUSH" OFF

127. **Jumbles:** LOVER FORTY TORRID NEWEST
Answer: Where the designer preferred the hemline—OVER TWO FEET

128. **Jumbles:** WAGON ICING BOTHER SHEKEL
Answer: Where did the clumsy dishwasher go?—ON HIS "BREAK"

129. **Jumbles:** LATCH GUILT EASILY INLAND
Answer: Winning the championship left the basketball team doing this—STANDING TALL

130. **Jumbles:** DELVE ONION VERIFY WOBBLE
Answer: How he felt when he rolled a perfect game—BOWLED OVER

131. **Jumbles:** FIORD ESSAY INFANT FLORAL
Answer: What the train engineers shared at their reunion—RAILROAD TIES

132. **Jumbles:** CAMEO FINIS DUPLEX INFECT
Answer: This can put your budget in disrepair—A "FIXED" INCOME

133. **Jumbles:** PLAID GAILY LEVITY WHENCE
Answer: What the homing pigeon did when it lost its way—"WINGED" IT

134. **Jumbles:** STEED LEAVE HALVED APATHY
Answer: What the crooked peddler offered on the sunny beach—A "SHADY" DEAL

135. **Jumbles:** LOUSE LEAKY BLUISH OPENLY
Answer: How the bartender felt at the end of his shift—ALL SHOOK UP

136. **Jumbles:** YOUNG MOURN LEAVEN TRUANT
Answer: What the actor hoped the play about a marathon would have—A LONG RUN

137. **Jumbles:** SPURN HASTY ECZEMA COUSIN
Answer: What he needed to do when he wanted the Halloween mask—SCARE UP CASH

138. **Jumbles:** EXCEL MILKY DREDGE ASSAIL
Answer: When he arrived for the hunt he was—DRESSED TO "KILL"

139. **Jumbles:** SWISH GRIPE VALISE FINITE
Answer: What a crash diet can lead to—"FAST" LIVING

140. **Jumbles:** NOBLE RIGOR NAUGHT PELVIS
Answer: What Mom came up with when the carpet was mysteriously stained—A "SOLUTION"

141. **Jumbles:** EAGLE GLEAM LAGOON THRASH
Answer: Served by the aspiring actor at the breakfast diner—"HAM" AND EGGS

142. **Jumbles:** MIRTH MUSTY SQUIRM UNLIKE
Answer: What Mom created when she used her new mixer—QUITE A STIR

143. **Jumbles:** NOISE GUIDE SNAPPY STRONG
    Answer: What the customer experienced when he visited the new pub—A GRAND "OPENING"

144. **Jumbles:** PLUME VALVE MALICE ENDURE
    Answer: When he was awakened early, his wife was—ALARMED

145. **Jumbles:** SNARL POISE GHETTO CARNAL
    Answer: What the kids turned Dad's van into—A "SPORTS" CAR

146. **Jumbles:** BRAWL AWFUL BUMPER DECEIT
    Answer: How the lioness felt when surrounded by her cubs—FULL OF "PRIDE"

147. **Jumbles:** BORAX SOUSE PREFIX TIDBIT
    Answer: What she did when she received a necklace from the pirate chest—"TREASURED" IT

148. **Jumbles:** FANCY HELLO SAVORY GAMBIT
    Answer: What the computer staff considered the break lounge—A CHAT ROOM

149. **Jumbles:** TESTY PAPER TRICKY NINETY
    Answer: What she gave him after her spill at the skating rink—AN "ICY" STARE

150. **Jumbles:** HITCH AIDED PETITE AROUSE
    Answer: A conversation at a sports bar can become this—"SPIRITED"

151. **Jumbles:** PILOT EMPTY SAVAGE SATIRE
    Answer: Why Junior didn't get any supper—IT WAS PAST REPAST

152. **Jumbles:** FLANK VYING MYSELF FUMBLE
    Answer: What the teen turned into when Mom asked the questions—A "YES" MAN

153. **Jumbles:** CHICK SCOUT JITNEY COUGAR
    Answer: Where medieval disputes were often settled—IN KNIGHT COURT

154. **Jumbles:** ABASH MAIZE OVERDO BUTLER
    Answer: When the boys cleared driveways after the storm they—SHOVELED IT IN

155. **Jumbles:** CHEEK AXIOM FACTOR CORRAL
    Answer: What the barbers were known as at the base—THE HAIR FORCE

156. **Jumbles:** AGONY LIMIT LIZARD INFLUX
    Answer: When the dentist made a pie, he excelled at this, naturally—THE FILLING

157. **Jumbles:** GNOME AORTA NIBBLE PUMICE
    Answer: What the fisherman wanted to increase—HIS "NET" INCOME

158. **Jumbles:** STUNG RODEO ORPHAN PALLID
    Answer: How he felt when Fido barked all night—DOG-TIRED

159. **Jumbles:** DRONE FLOOR POPLAR FRENZY
    Answer: What he did when he couldn't fix the ceiling leak—"RAZED" THE ROOF

160. **Jumbles:** BURST WAGER CANINE MEMBER
    Answer: The audience found the cop's performance as an actor—"ARRESTING"

161. **Jumbles:** DECENT BISECT SCHOOL MISFIT CHARGE HAZING
    Answer: When the couple got silverware as a wedding gift, they said it was a—"STERLING" CHOICE

162. **Jumbles:** JUMBLE CRABBY EMBRYO HARDLY RAGLAN FABLED
    Answer: To succeed, the wine merchant needed a—BUYER AND A "CELLAR"

163. **Jumbles:** WEDGED AVOWAL JOYFUL EVOLVE TYPIST CHROME
    Answer: When the check came for his juicy, tender steak, it was—TOUGH TO SWALLOW

164. **Jumbles:** BEAUTY TARGET TURBAN RABBIT WHEEZE JIGGLE
    Answer: During rounds, the cardiologist gave his patient a—"HEARTY" GREETING

165. **Jumbles:** FROZEN QUIVER DABBLE HEIFER EMBALM BESIDE
    Answer: Where the poet ended up going during the course of his career—FROM BAD TO "VERSE"

166. **Jumbles:** APIECE FUNGUS POUNCE ENOUGH POETIC COWARD
    Answer: When Junior volunteered to clean the house, Mom said it was a—"SWEEPING" CHANGE

167. **Jumbles:** INBORN GARBLE STUDIO IMBIBE ORATOR AMAZON
    Answer: The TV chef turned the cooking show into this—A "STIRRING" DRAMA

168. **Jumbles:** FAIRLY TREATY CORNEA AIRWAY OFFSET PIRACY
    Answer: What the mailman's dog turned into when she had puppies—A LITTER CARRIER

169. **Jumbles:** UNLESS SOCIAL BEWARE HERESY AMPERE DAMAGE
    Answer: Avoided by the exotic dancer—A "DRESS" REHEARSAL

170. **Jumbles:** FORMAT PAROLE EFFORT PRYING NESTLE SUBWAY
    Answer: What the sudden rain did to the picnickers—"WET" THEIR APPETITES

171. **Jumbles:** BOILED LIQUOR SCURVY MORTAR GUIDED ENGULF
    Answer: They bet on the same horse because they were—"MUTUEL" FRIENDS

172. **Jumbles:** WOEFUL MEMORY VANDAL BURLAP FORGER POORLY
    Answer: How the butcher got ahead in his job—FROM THE "GROUND" UP

173. **Jumbles:** BEDBUG HECKLE CHOSEN SALUTE GENIUS NOGGIN
    Answer: What the shop owner did when the hunter made him an offer—STUCK TO HIS GUNS

174. **Jumbles:** LACKEY FONDLY GADFLY HELIUM ATOMIC HAGGLE
    Answer: Why she gave her husband a massage—TO FULFILL A "KNEAD"

175. **Jumbles:** ASTRAY CANOPY BRAZEN VANISH FORMAL JUNIOR
    Answer: What the sulky driver wanted to do when he led the race—"HARNESS" VICTORY

176. **Jumbles:** SURELY JAILED DULCET TOWARD BEHIND BYWORD
    Answer: What the referee became when the teams got unruly—A WHISTLE-BLOWER

177. **Jumbles:** BLOODY SPONGE DUGOUT GUZZLE CANYON MOHAIR
    Answer: When the butcher was late for dinner, his wife gave him this—THE COLD "SHOULDER"

178. **Jumbles:** BUTTER BUTANE AROUND LICHEN RAREFY RECTOR
    Answer: The sociologist joined the regulars at the coffee shop to study the—"COUNTER" CULTURE

179. **Jumbles:** GOLFER SOOTHE PUSHER MILDEW GENDER FRACAS
    Answer: This happened when the nursery's sales increased—PROFITS FLOWERED

180. **Jumbles:** VACANT MYOPIC CONVOY FROSTY TRICKY ADROIT
    Answer: What the disc jockey did with his new car—TOOK IT FOR A "SPIN"

Need More Jumbles®?

Jumble® Books
More than 175 puzzles each!

Animal Jumble®
$9.95 • ISBN: 1-57243-197-0

Jammin' Jumble®
$9.95 • ISBN: 1-57243-844-4

Jazzy Jumble®
$9.95 • ISBN: 978-1-57243-962-7

Jumble® at Work
$9.95 • ISBN: 1-57243-147-4

Joyful Jumble®
$9.95 • ISBN: 978-1-60078-079-0

Jumble® Celebration
$9.95 • ISBN: 978-1-60078-134-6

Jumble® Explosion
$9.95 • ISBN: 978-1-60078-078-3

Jumble® Fever
$9.95 • ISBN: 1-57243-593-3

Jumble® Fiesta
$9.95 • ISBN: 1-57243-626-3

Jumble® Fun
$9.95 • ISBN: 1-57243-379-5

Jumble® Genius
$9.95 • ISBN: 1-57243-896-7

Jumble® Grab Bag
$9.95 • ISBN: 1-57243-273-X

Jumble® Jackpot
$9.95 • ISBN: 1-57243-897-5

Jumble® Jamboree
$9.95 • ISBN: 1-57243-696-4

Jumble® Jubilee
$9.95 • ISBN: 1-57243-231-4

Jumble® Juggernaut
$9.95 • ISBN: 978-1-60078-026-4

Jumble® Junction
$9.95 • ISBN: 1-57243-380-9

Jumble® Jungle
$9.95 • ISBN: 978-1-57243-961-0

Jumble® Madness
$9.95 • ISBN: 1-892049-24-4

Jumble® Mania
$9.95 • ISBN: 1-57243-697-2

Jumble® See & Search
$9.95 • ISBN: 1-57243-549-6

Jumble® See & Search 2
$9.95 • ISBN: 1-57243-734-0

Jumble® Surprise
$9.95 • ISBN: 1-57243-320-5

Jumble® Junction
$9.95 • ISBN: 1-57243-380-9

Jumpin' Jumble®
$9.95 • ISBN: 978-1-60078-027-1

Ready, Set, Jumble®
$9.95 • ISBN: 978-1-60078-133-0

Sports Jumble®
$9.95 • ISBN: 1-57243-113-X

Summer Fun Jumble®
$9.95 • ISBN: 1-57243-114-8

Travel Jumble®
$9.95 • ISBN: 1-57243-198-9

TV Jumble®
$9.95 • ISBN: 1-57243-461-9

Oversize Jumble® Books
More than 500 puzzles each!

Colossal Jumble®
$19.95 • ISBN: 1-57243-490-2

Generous Jumble®
$19.95 • ISBN: 1-57243-385-X

Giant Jumble®
$19.95 • ISBN: 1-57243-349-3

Gigantic Jumble®
$19.95 • ISBN: 1-57243-426-0

Jumbo Jumble®
$19.95 • ISBN: 1-57243-314-0

The Very Best of Jumble® BrainBusters
$19.95 • ISBN: 1-57243-845-2

Jumble® Crosswords™
More than 175 puzzles each!

Jumble® Crosswords™
$9.95 • ISBN: 1-57243-347-7

More Jumble® Crosswords™
$9.95 • ISBN: 1-57243-386-8

Jumble® Crosswords™ Adventure
$9.95 • ISBN: 1-57243-462-7

Jumble® Crosswords™ Challenge
$9.95 • ISBN: 1-57243-423-6

Jumble® Crosswords™ Jackpot
$9.95 • ISBN: 1-57243-615-8

Jumble® Crosswords™ Jamboree
$9.95 • ISBN: 1-57243-787-1

Jumble® BrainBusters™
More than 175 puzzles each!

Jumble® BrainBusters™
$9.95 • ISBN: 1-892049-28-7

Jumble® BrainBusters™ II
$9.95 • ISBN: 1-57243-424-4

Jumble® BrainBusters™ III
$9.95 • ISBN: 1-57243-463-5

Jumble® BrainBusters™ IV
$9.95 • ISBN: 1-57243-489-9

Jumble® BrainBusters™ 5
$9.95 • ISBN: 1-57243-548-8

Hollywood Jumble® BrainBusters™
$9.95 • ISBN: 1-57243-594-1

Jumble® BrainBusters™ Bonanza
$9.95 • ISBN: 1-57243-616-6

Boggle™ BrainBusters™
$9.95 • ISBN: 1-57243-592-5

Boggle™ BrainBusters™ 2
$9.95 • ISBN: 1-57243-788-X

Jumble® BrainBusters™ Junior
$9.95 • ISBN: 1-892049-29-5

Jumble® BrainBusters™ Junior II
$9.95 • ISBN: 1-57243-425-2

Fun in the Sun with Jumble® BrainBusters™
$9.95 • ISBN: 1-57243-733-2